GRAMMAR TO Go **3**

ENGLISH GRAMMAR PRACTICE

ROBERT J. DIXSON

Longman

longman.com

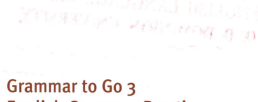

Grammar to Go 3
English Grammar Practice

Pearson Education, 10 Bank Street, White Plains, NY 10606

Executive editor: Laura Le Dréan
Associate acquisitions editor: Dena Daniel
Development editors: Katherine Rawson, Tara Maldonado
Senior production editor: Kathleen Silloway
Production editor: Diana P. George
Marketing manager: Joe Chapple
Senior manufacturing buyer: David Dickey
Cover and interior design: Tracey Munz Cataldo
Text composition: Laserwords
Text font: MetaPlusBook 11/14

Library of Congress Cataloging-in-Publication Data

Dixson, Robert James.
    Grammar to go : English grammar practice / Robert J. Dixson.
       p. cm.
    ISBN 0-13-118283-8 (bk. 1)—ISBN 0-13-118284-6 (bk. 2)—ISBN 0-13-118285-4 (bk. 3)
    1. English language—Grammar—Problems, exercises, etc. I. Title.
    PE1112.D595 2004
    428.2'076—dc22

                                                                                    2004005980

ISBN: 0-13-118285-4

Printed in the United States of America
   2 3 4 5 6 7 8 9 10—BAH—09 08 07 06 05 04

There is no need here to describe the different types of exercises that this book contains or to discuss their wide variety and extent. A glance through the following pages is enough to acquaint anyone with the book's general contents.

Since this is a workbook, there is also little to say as to how it should be used. Each exercise carries its own instructions, and the students proceed accordingly. On the other hand, there are a few points of general pedagogy that the teacher using the book should keep in mind.

First, this is a workbook, and all explanatory material has been kept to a minimum. Thus, the book is not designed to be used alone or to replace completely the regular classroom text. Rather, this book should be used to supplement the regular classroom text, to give needed variety to the lesson, or to provide additional drill materials on important points of grammar and usage.

Second, as a teacher using this book, don't assume that after students have written the answers to an exercise correctly, they know the material thoroughly and can use the principle in their everyday speech. The exercise is often only the beginning. Much drill and practice are still necessary. Therefore, ask questions or introduce simple conversation involving the particular grammar principle. Also, don't hesitate to repeat the exercises in the book several times. Run over these exercises orally in class. If the students have already written the answers in their books, they can cover these answers with their hand or with a separate sheet of paper. Continue to review past exercises that seem important to you or that have given the students difficulty.

Third, don't fall into the further error of assuming that some of the exercises in this book are too easy for your particular students. Certain exercises may seem easy to you—especially if you speak English as a native—but they still represent a real challenge to anyone learning English. With this in mind, there is one additional point of utmost importance to consider. We are not interested in tricking or even in testing the student with these exercises. That is, the exercises are not designed to find out how much a student knows or does not know. Their purpose is simply to drill the student on certain basic points of grammar and usage. The exercises are practice exercises—nothing more. For this reason, the exercises have been made as simple and as clear as possible. For the same reason, a good deal of direct repetition has been purposely introduced, not only in individual exercises but throughout the book.

There are three books in this series. *Grammar to Go 1* is for the beginning student; *Grammar to Go 2* is for the intermediate student; *Grammar to Go 3* is for the advanced student. The **Grammar to Go** series is readily adaptable to many uses and can serve effectively to supplement any standard classroom textbook. A perforated answer key at the back of the book makes classroom use or self-study equally feasible.

R.J.D.

CONTENTS

Full Form	Contraction	Full Form	Contraction
I am	I'm	we are	we're
you are	you're	you are	you're
he is	he's	they are	they're
she is	she's		
it is	it's		

A. Fill in the blank using the correct form of the present tense of to be. *Use the contracted form.*

1. _____*She's*_____ a good student. (she)

2. _____ good friends. (they)

3. _____ a beautiful day. (it)

4. _____ absent today. (he)

5. _____ good news. (it)

6. _____ brothers. (we)

7. _____ a doctor. (she)

8. _____ a foreign student. (I)

9. _____ a foreign student. (you)

10. _____ foreign students. (they)

B. Fill in the blank with the correct form of the present tense of to be. *Use the full form.*

1. He _____*is*_____ a good student.

2. Sheila _____ a business executive.

3. Today _____ Monday.

4. She and Taro _____ both good students.

5. The police officer _____ busy with the traffic.

6. He and I _____ old friends.

7. These books _____ yours.

8. Yellow _____ my favorite color.

9. Spring _____ a beautiful time of year.

TO BE

Present Tense: Negative and Question Forms

Form questions by placing the verb before the subject. Form the negative by placing *not* after the verb. The contractions are *aren't* and *isn't*.

Is she a lawyer?	**No, she isn't a lawyer.**

Change the statement to the question form. Then give a negative answer.

1. They're in Europe now.

   a. *Are they in Europe now?*

   b. *They aren't in Europe now.*

2. Ricardo is angry with us.

   a. _____

   b. _____

3. Maya and Anna are good friends.

   a. _____

   b. _____

4. He is very happy.

   a. _____

   b. _____

5. Both sisters are tall and athletic.

   a. _____

   b. _____

6. She is a clever girl.

   a. _____

   b. _____

7. They are members of our club.

   a. _____

   b. _____

8. He is a good baseball player.

   a. _____

   b. _____

I was	we were
you were	you were
he was	they were
she was	
it was	

Fill in the blank with the correct past tense form of to be.

1. Carlos _____*was*_____ absent from school last week.

2. I _____ in the same class as Sally last year.

3. We _____ good friends for many years.

4. The windows of the car _____ open.

5. Both doors _____ closed.

6. Mike _____ not at work yesterday.

7. They _____ sick.

8. You _____ not at home last night when I called.

9. We _____ tired after our long walk.

10. I _____ hungry after so much work.

11. There _____ many students absent yesterday.

12. She _____ present at the lesson, but I _____ not.

13. The weather _____ very warm yesterday.

14. He _____ at his aunt's house all day.

15. The teacher _____ satisfied with my composition.

16. The exercises in the last lesson _____ easy.

17. We _____ happy to hear the good news.

18. The wind last night _____ very strong.

19. It _____ cold last night.

20. We _____ happy to hear the good news.

21. When I saw her, she _____ very happy.

22. Her face _____ full of happiness.

23. We _____ thrilled to hear about her success.

24. We ate the apples and thought they _____ delicious.

Past Tense: Negative and Question Forms

Form questions by placing the verb before the subject. Form the negative by placing *not* after the verb. The contractions are *wasn't* and *weren't*.

> **Was she a doctor?**   **She wasn't a doctor.**

Change the statement to the question form. Then give a negative answer.

1. He was absent yesterday.

   a. *Was he absent yesterday?*

   b. *He wasn't absent yesterday.*

2. The doors were closed.

   a. _____

   b. _____

3. The exercises were difficult.

   a. _____

   b. _____

4. The woman was a stranger to her.

   a. _____

   b. _____

5. It was a beautiful day.

   a. _____

   b. _____

6. The sea was very calm.

   a. _____

   b. _____

7. He was a tall man.

   a. _____

   b. _____

8. There were many difficult exercises in the lesson.

   a. _____

   b. _____

The present continuous tense describes an action that is going on at the moment of speaking and is not yet complete. Form the present continuous tense with the present tense of the verb *to be* and the present participle of the main verb.

I am (I'm) working.	We are (We're) working.
You are (You're) working.	You are (You're) working.
He is (He's) working.	They are (They're) working.
She is (She's) working.	
It is (It's) working.	

Fill in the blank using the present continuous form of the verb in parentheses. Use the contracted form with personal pronouns.

1. _____*They're waiting*_____ for us downstairs. (they, wait)

2. The bus _____ for us now. (stop)

3. I think the telephone _____. (ring)

4. I see that _____ your new suit today. (you, wear)

5. Look! A deer _____ the road. (cross)

6. Listen! Someone _____ a car. (start)

7. Please be quiet! The baby _____. (sleep)

8. Look! The cat _____ to climb that tall tree. (try)

9. Muna _____ good progress in her studies. (make)

10. The leaves _____ to fall from the trees. (begin)

11. Bertha _____ lunch in the cafeteria now. (have)

12. Listen! Pat _____ the piano. (play)

13. At present, _____ in South America. (they, live)

14. For the time being, Jack _____ this department. (manage)

15. Be careful! The teacher _____ you. (watch)

16. _____ sales in all the department stores now. (they, have)

17. Mother _____ the garden now. (water)

18. The Salazar family _____ the summer in Venezuela. (spend)

PRESENT CONTINUOUS TENSE

Negative and Question Forms

Form questions in the present continuous tense by placing *to be* before the subject. Form negatives in the present continuous tense by placing *not* after *to be*.

Is Daniel studying tonight?	**No, he isn't studying tonight.**

Change the statement to the question form. Then give a negative answer.

1. The telephone is ringing.

   a. _Is the telephone ringing?_ _____

   b. _The telephone isn't ringing._ _____

2. It is beginning to rain.

   a. _____

   b. _____

3. The sky is growing dark.

   a. _____

   b. _____

4. He is working for a new company.

   a. _____

   b. _____

5. Pete is cleaning the room now.

   a. _____

   b. _____

6. The joggers are turning the corner.

   a. _____

   b. _____

7. She is having lunch outside on the patio.

   a. _____

   b. _____

8. Nora is doing well in college.

   a. _____

   b. _____

The past continuous tense describes an action in the past that was going on when another action took place. Form the past continuous tense with the past tense of *to be* and the present participle of the main verb.

> I was working. We were working.
>
> You were working. You were working.
>
> He was working. They were working.
>
> She was working.
>
> It was working.

Fill in the blank with the past continuous form of the verb in parentheses.

1. They _____ *were eating* _____ in the restaurant when we called. (eat)

2. It _____ when I left home. (rain)

3. When you telephoned, I _____ dinner. (have)

4. They _____ in Europe when the storm hit. (travel)

5. The baby _____ soundly when the telephone rang. (sleep)

6. He _____ breakfast when I went to his hotel room. (order)

7. I got sick while we _____ to Mexico. (drive)

8. He _____ in California when his father died. (work)

9. I _____ a nap when you called. (take)

10. She _____ with Mr. Wong when I saw her in the hall. (talk)

11. The accident happened while they _____ in a hotel. (stay)

12. She fell as she _____ into a taxi. (get)

13. The car _____ slowly when it struck the dog. (go)

14. When I got up this morning, the sun _____ brightly. (shine)

15. Annette _____ TV when the storm began. (watch)

16. My parents _____ to the store when their car died. (drive)

17. As the student left the room, he _____ a paper ball. (throw)

18. While we smelled the flowers, Luisa _____. (sneeze)

FUTURE CONTINUOUS TENSE

The future continuous tense describes an action that will be going on in the future.
Form the future continuous tense with the future tense of the verb *to be* and the present participle of the main verb.

I will (I'll) be working.	We will (We'll) be working.
You will (You'll) be working.	You will (You'll) be working.
He will (He'll) be working.	They will (They'll) be working.
She will (She'll) be working.	
It will (It'll) be working.	

Fill in the blank using the future continuous form of the verb in parentheses. Use the contracted form with personal pronouns.

1. If you come at noon, _____*we'll be eating*_____ lunch. (we, eat)

2. At this time next month, _____ in India. (John, travel)

3. At ten o'clock tomorrow morning, _____ my music lesson. (I, have)

4. _____ for you on the corner at the usual time tomorrow morning. (I, wait)

5. If you call her at 6:00, _____ the piano. (she, practice)

6. _____ when you get back. (it, rain)

7. If you arrive before 5:00, _____ in my garden. (I, work)

8. Tomorrow afternoon at this time, _____ over the Caribbean Sea. (we, fly)

9. Don't call him between seven and eight. _____ his favorite TV show. (he, watch)

10. Don't call her before four. _____ her usual afternoon nap. (she, take)

11. At this time next year, _____ at Columbia University. (he, study)

12. If we go there now, _____ dinner. (my parents, have)

13. But if we go later, _____ TV. (they, watch)

14. At this time tomorrow afternoon, _____ my final English exam. (I, take)

15. On Saturday, _____ home. (my brother and I, drive)

The simple present tense describes an action that goes on every day or in general.

I work.	We work.
You work.	You work.
He works.	They work.
She works.	
It works.	

Fill in the blank with the present tense form of the verb in parentheses.

1. We _____read_____ the newspaper every day. (read)
2. He _____ to school by bus. (come)
3. I always _____ to school. (walk)
4. The children _____ in the park every afternoon. (play)
5. I _____ lunch in the cafeteria every day. (eat)
6. Sue _____ very hard. (work)
7. I _____ to sit in the sun. (like)
8. The dog _____ the cat all around the house. (chase)
9. Ms. Glenfield _____ at the clinic. (work)
10. Joan generally _____ at this desk. (sit)
11. We always _____ tennis on Saturdays. (play)
12. He always _____ his homework carefully. (prepare)
13. They _____ lunch together every day. (eat)
14. My son _____ to play video games. (like)
15. They _____ many trips together. (take)
16. We always _____ by car. (travel)
17. Eric _____ his grandmother every Friday. (visit)
18. She _____ several foreign languages. (speak)
19. They _____ to the park as often as they can. (go)
20. He _____ the garden every day. (water)
21. My boss _____ every morning before work. (jog)
22. She _____ her mind often. (change)

SIMPLE PRESENT TENSE

Negative Form

Form the negative of the simple present tense by placing *do not* or *does not* before the simple form of the verb. The contractions are *don't* and *doesn't*.

> I do not (don't) know.   He does not (doesn't) know.

A. *Change the statement to the negative form. Use the full form.*

1. I work on the tenth floor.

   I do not work on the tenth floor.

2. Ann likes to study English.

   _____

3. They speak Chinese well.

   _____

4. The plane leaves at ten o'clock.

   _____

5. He knows French perfectly.

   _____

6. I live in this neighborhood.

   _____

B. *Change the statement to the negative form. Use the contracted form.*

1. They live in Chicago.

   They don't live in Chicago.

2. I need air conditioning in my room.

   _____

3. We read a lot of books every summer.

   _____

4. I understand everything he says.

   _____

5. She wants to visit Mexico.

   _____

6. Sara enjoys classical music.

   _____

Form questions in the simple present tense by placing *do* or *does* before the subject. Use the simple form of the main verb.

Do I go?	Do we go?
Do you go?	Do you go?
Does he go?	Do they go?
Does she go?	
Does it go?	

Change the statement to the question form.

1. They speak English well.

   Do they speak English well?

2. He enjoys fishing.

   _____

3. She spends her vacation in the mountains.

   _____

4. They come to school by bus.

   _____

5. Andrew knows how to play soccer.

   _____

6. The children wake up at six o'clock every morning.

   _____

7. He knows a lot about politics.

   _____

8. They go to the park every afternoon.

   _____

9. They have many friends in that school.

   _____

10. Both boys swim well.

    _____

11. They live on the outskirts of the city.

    _____

REGULAR VERBS

Past Tense

The past tense describes an action that occurred at a definite time in the past. Form the past tense of regular verbs by adding *ed* to the simple form of the verb.

I worked.	We worked.
You worked.	You worked.
He worked.	They worked.
She worked.	
It worked.	

Fill in the blank with the past tense form of the verb in parentheses.

1. We _____worked_____ in our garden yesterday. (work)

2. I _____ to the radio until twelve o'clock last night. (listen)

3. Yoshiko and I _____ by telephone yesterday. (talk)

4. He always _____ to learn English. (want)

5. They _____ in Sydney for many years. (live)

6. We _____ to go to Europe last June. (expect)

7. The meeting _____ about two hours. (last)

8. Mrs. Walker _____ trains in New York. (change)

9. We both _____ the movie last night very much. (like)

10. I _____ almost two hours for Tom and Lynn. (wait)

11. They _____ their house white. (paint)

12. Daniel _____ late for class. (arrive)

13. We _____ TV until eleven o'clock last night. (watch)

14. She _____ in our class last semester. (study)

15. I _____ your letter on my way to work. (mail)

16. We both _____ how to swim many years ago. (learn)

17. The boy _____ the groceries early in the morning. (deliver)

18. Carol _____ all the way to the store. (walk)

19. Mother _____ a wonderful dinner last night. (cook)

20. I _____ to her as she got on the bus. (wave)

21. Josh _____ his final exam. (pass)

22. He _____ the radio and went to sleep. (turn off)

23. They _____ to another town. (move)

You must memorize the past tense form for irregular verbs. See the appendix for a longer list of irregular verbs.

begin → began	go → went	see → saw
come → came	have → had	sit → sat
cost → cost	hear → heard	sell → sold
drink → drank	know → knew	speak → spoke
feel → felt	put → put	tell → told
give → gave	read → read	write → wrote

Fill in the blank with the past tense form of the verb in parentheses.

1. Ms. Burns ____*came*____ to visit us last night. (come)

2. They _____ us about their plans for the new home. (tell)

3. The weather was pleasant, so we _____ on our front porch. (sit)

4. I _____ your hat and coat in the next room. (put)

5. Last night the meeting _____ at 8:00 and ended at 10:00. (begin)

6. I stayed home last night and _____ several e-mail messages. (write)

7. He _____ Angela on the street yesterday. (see)

8. This book _____ two dollars. (cost)

9. I _____ my lunch in the cafeteria at noon. (have)

10. The man _____ a lot of water after the race. (drink)

11. I _____ John your message. (give)

12. Mrs. Reese finally _____ her house. (sell)

13. Anne _____ the president speak on TV last night. (hear)

14. My father _____ Mr. Evans well. (know)

15. Dolores _____ well yesterday, but today she feels sick again. (feel)

16. We _____ to the park yesterday. (go)

17. I _____ that novel several years ago. (read)

18. She _____ to me as soon as she _____ in. (speak, come)

19. Dennis _____ her the news. (tell)

Negative Form

Form the negative in the past tense by placing *did not* before the simple form of the verb. The contraction is *didn't*.

> **I did not work.   (I didn't work.)**

A. *Change the statement to the negative form using the full form* did not.

1. He wrote his report on the computer.

   He did not write his report on the computer.

2. They faxed us the story.

   _____

3. She put the bank statements on his desk.

   _____

4. We stayed in Mexico City for two weeks.

   _____

5. I saw Florence yesterday.

   _____

B. *Change the statement to the negative form using the contraction* didn't.

1. The man fainted in the heat.

   The man didn't faint in the heat.

2. I knew him very well.

   _____

3. You sold your new modem.

   _____

4. Mr. Wood spoke to Beth about the exam.

   _____

5. She came to the meeting alone.

   _____

6. We sat together at the concert last night.

   _____

Form questions in the past tense by placing *did* before the subject. Use the simple form of the verb.

Did I work?	**Did we work?**
Did you work?	**Did you work?**
Did he work?	**Did they work?**
Did she work?	
Did it work?	

Change the statement to the question form.

1. She worked all day.

   Did she work all day?

2. Don gave her some CDs for her birthday.

   _____

3. They stayed in Japan all year.

   _____

4. She told us about her trip.

   _____

5. He began his university classes in September.

   _____

6. They went by plane.

   _____

7. She came home very late.

   _____

8. They went to the party together.

   _____

9. They knew each other as children.

   _____

10. Rose worked there for many years.

    _____

11. Mr. Stein felt better after his surgery.

    _____

FUTURE TENSE

The future tense expresses promise or determination. Form the future tense by placing *will* before the simple form of the verb.

I will (I'll) go.	We will (We'll) go.
You will (You'll) go.	You will (You'll) go.
He will (He'll) go.	They will (They'll) go.
She will (She'll) go.	
It will (It'll) go.	

Fill in the blank using the future tense form of the verb in parentheses. Use the contracted form with personal pronouns.

1. _____He'll call_____ you tomorrow. (he, call)
2. _____ us in the morning. (they, see)
3. _____ you that money tomorrow. (I, give)
4. _____ you with that project. (she, help)
5. John _____ the table right away. (clean)
6. The mall _____ early today. (close)
7. _____ the tip. (I, leave)
8. Barbara _____ the file that you need. (find)
9. _____ a place to stay. (you, need)
10. Kevin _____ well in that job. (do)
11. The wind _____ that sign down. (blow)
12. _____ you in Grand Central Station. (we, meet)
13. _____ the bill. (I, pay)
14. _____ a great deal in that course. (you, learn)
15. _____ in Mexico about a month. (we, remain)
16. Her secretary says that _____ back at six o'clock. (she, be)
17. Sonia _____ the cashier. (pay)
18. _____ a lot of money there. (you, spend)
19. _____ you a cup of tea. (I, make)
20. I'm sure _____ the book you lost. (you, find)
21. My boss _____ me a raise next week. (give)
22. The stores _____ at nine o'clock. (open)

Form negatives in the future tense by placing *not* after *will* or by using the contraction *won't* before the main verb.

> **I will not go.**   **(I won't go.)**

A. *Change the statement to the negative form using the full form* will not.

1. They will arrive at three o'clock.

   They will not arrive at three o'clock.

2. My girlfriend will finish her degree next year.

   _____

3. I will be back tomorrow.

   _____

4. The weather will be cool tomorrow.

   _____

5. Tom will be able to meet us this evening.

   _____

B. *Change the statement to the negative form using the contraction* won't.

1. You will be there before dawn.

   You won't be there before dawn.

2. She will do well in that course.

   _____

3. Gina will teach all the computer courses.

   _____

4. Jim and I will sign the contract tomorrow.

   _____

5. They will finish the work in April.

   _____

6. The meeting will last an hour.

   _____

FUTURE TENSE

Question Form

Form questions in the future tense by placing *will* before the subject.

Will I go?	**Will we go?**
Will you go?	**Will you go?**
Will he go?	**Will they go?**
Will she go?	
Will it go?	

To use a question word, such as *where, when,* or *why,* place it before *will.*

Where will you go?	**When will he go?**	**Why will they go?**

A. *Change the statement to the question form.*

1. They will arrive on Wednesday.

   Will they arrive on Wednesday?

2. Ned will come back at three o'clock.

   _____

3. The shop will be open at six o'clock.

   _____

4. It will cost sixty dollars to fix the microwave.

   _____

5. The plant will die without sunshine.

   _____

B. *Form questions using the question words in parentheses.*

1. She will meet us somewhere. (Where)

   Where will she meet us?

2. They will pay their bill soon. (When)

   _____

3. The meeting will begin late. (What time)

   _____

4. The fireworks will last a while. (How long)

   _____

5. Lucy will buy something for her husband. (What)

   _____

The *going to* future describes future plans. Form the *going to* future with the appropriate form of *to be going to* and the simple form of the verb.

> I am (I'm) going to work.
> You are (You're) going to work.
> He is (He's) going to work.
> She is (She's) going to work.
> It is (It's) going to work.
>
> We are (We're) going to work.
> You are (You're) going to work.
> They are (They're) going to work.

Fill in the blank with the going to *future form of the verb in parentheses. Use the contracted form with personal pronouns.*

1. They _____'re going to visit_____ us tomorrow. (visit)

2. We _____ dinner in town tonight. (have)

3. I _____ to Disneyland this summer. (go)

4. He _____ for New York in the morning. (leave)

5. She _____ her family in Virginia. (visit)

6. You _____ at the meeting tonight. (speak)

7. Danny _____ Russian next year. (study)

8. Andrew _____ an exam on Wednesday. (take)

9. They _____ for us after the movie. (wait)

10. We _____ to Chicago. (fly)

11. Pedro _____ to be a doctor. (study)

12. We _____ up early tomorrow and go fishing. (get)

13. Mr. and Mrs. Park _____ to Canada on their vacation. (go)

14. She _____ for Europe soon. (leave)

15. They _____ that whole block of buildings. (tear down)

16. Joan _____ to town to buy some new clothes. (go)

17. They _____ their present home and buy a new one. (sell)

18. Mrs. Jacobs _____ her children to the zoo today. (take)

19. They _____ some new clothes for their vacation. (buy)

20. The children _____ their chores after breakfast. (do)

21. Their father _____ them. (help)

Negative and Question Forms

Form negatives in the *going to* future by placing *not* after *to be*.

> I'm not going to listen.
>
> They're not going to buy it.

Form questions in the *going to* future by placing *to be* before the subject.

> Are you going to have lunch?
>
> Is she going to come with us?

Change the statement to the question form. Then give a negative answer. Use the contracted form with personal pronouns.

1. They are going to wait for us.

    a. *Are they going to wait for us?*

    b. *They're not going to wait for us.*

2. Rose is going to take a vacation.

    a. _____

    b. _____

3. We are going to go to the movies tonight.

    a. _____

    b. _____

4. He is going to start working there on Monday.

    a. _____

    b. _____

5. They are going to pay him a good salary.

    a. _____

    b. _____

6. Carmen is going to move to California next month.

    a. _____

    b. _____

7. Henry is going to travel to Asia on business.

    a. _____

    b. _____

8. She is going to spend the weekend in Connecticut.

    a. _____

    b. _____

The present perfect tense describes a past action connected with the present time. Form the present perfect tense by placing *have* or *has* before the past participle of the verb.

I have (I've) worked.	We have (We've) worked.
You have (You've) worked.	You have (You've) worked.
He has (He's) worked.	They have (They've) worked.
She has (She's) worked.	
It has (It's) worked.	

Fill in the blank with the present perfect form of the verb in parentheses. Use the contracted form with personal pronouns.

1. I _____'ve spoken_____ to him about it several times. (speak)
2. We _____ our homework. (finish)
3. He _____ us many times. (visit)
4. She _____ my book at last. (return)
5. I am afraid that I _____ my car keys. (lose)
6. We _____ to Mexico many times. (be)
7. I _____ this exercise before. (do)
8. We _____ many new words in this course. (learn)
9. Mr. and Mrs. Santini _____ to Montreal. (be)
10. I _____ that story before. (hear)
11. We _____ money to them several times. (lend)
12. Mr. Petridis _____ to work in South America. (go)
13. His uncle _____ computer science for years. (teach)
14. She _____ that movie three times. (see)
15. Kelly _____ that recipe many times. (try)
16. He _____ to understand what Alice wants. (begin)
17. The flowers _____ very high. (grew)
18. They _____ to Hawaii many times. (be)
19. Otto _____ them in Mexico twice. (visit)

PRESENT PERFECT TENSE

Negative and Question Forms

Form questions with the present perfect tense by placing *have* or *has* before the subject. Form the negative of the present perfect tense by placing *not* after *have* or *has*. The contractions are *haven't* and *hasn't*.

Has he seen it?   **He hasn't seen it.**

Change the statement to the question form. Then give a negative answer. Use the contracted form of have *or* has + not.

1. He has worked very hard.

   a. *Has he worked very hard?*

   b. *He hasn't worked very hard.*

2. She has been there for many years.

   a. _____

   b. _____

3. They have waited there a long time.

   a. _____

   b. _____

4. The movie has been seen by millions of people.

   a. _____

   b. _____

5. Mr. and Mrs. Sato have studied English.

   a. _____

   b. _____

6. Alan has been absent.

   a. _____

   b. _____

7. They have found the money.

   a. _____

   b. _____

8. He has been the best student all year.

   a. _____

   b. _____

Form the present perfect continuous tense by placing *have* or *has* or its contracted form before *been* plus the present participle of the verb.

I have (I've) been working.	We have (We've) been working.
You have (You've) been working.	You have (You've) been working.
He has (He's) been working.	They have (They've) been working.
She has (She's) been working.	
It has (It's) been working.	

The present perfect continuous tense can often be used interchangeably with the present perfect tense when expressing an action that started in the past and continues to the present.

Change the statement to the present perfect continuous tense. Use the contracted form with personal pronouns.

1. She has worked there for many years.

   She's been working there for many years.

2. He has sold cars for many years.

   _____

3. They have lived in Europe since last spring.

   _____

4. Susan has slept for more than ten hours.

   _____

5. It has rained all day long.

   _____

6. My brother has studied English for many years.

   _____

7. She has caught fish in that stream for years.

   _____

8. He has taught English for ten years.

   _____

9. The two nations have quarreled for many years.

   _____

PAST PERFECT TENSE

The past perfect tense describes an action that took place before a definite time or action in the past. It is often used with the past tense. Form the past perfect tense by placing *had ('d)* before the past participle of the verb. *Had* can be contracted with all the personal pronouns except *it*.

I had (I'd) gone.	We had (We'd) gone.
You had (You'd) gone.	You had (You'd) gone.
He had (He'd) gone.	They had (They'd) gone.
She had (She'd) gone.	
It had gone.	

Fill in the blank with the past perfect form of the verb in parentheses.

1. The professor _____ *had left* _____ by the time we arrived. (leave)

2. He told me that he _____ everywhere for us. (look)

3. Before coming to us, he _____ in sales. (work)

4. Roberta told me that the police _____ the thief. (caught)

5. The teacher returned the exercises we _____ for her. (prepare)

6. The package was late because we _____ the wrong address. (write)

7. I met them before I _____ a hundred yards. (go)

8. He _____ there for just a week when the accident happened. (work)

9. When I got to the restaurant, my friends _____ dinner already. (order)

10. They told me that Henry _____ the class. (leave)

11. She insisted that she _____ that movie. (see)

12. When I got off the bus, it _____ raining. (stop)

13. Richard _____ the news by the time I saw him. (heard)

14. Previously, he _____ a very good student. (be)

15. It was clear that someone _____ us. (misdirect)

16. Shirley and Roger _____ married for several years when they bought their house. (be)

17. Harry _____ several countries before coming here. (visit)

18. Amina wasn't hungry because she _____ a big lunch. (eat)

19. By the time I finished writing the report, the deadline _____. (pass)

20. By the time Chris served the cake, many of the guests _____. (leave)

The past perfect continuous tense describes a continuing action that ended before another action in the past. Form the past perfect continuous tense by placing *had been* before the present participle of the verb.

I had (I'd) been working.	We had (We'd) been working.
You had (You'd) been working.	You had (You'd) been working.
He had (He'd) been working.	They had (They'd) been working.
She had (She'd) been working.	

Fill in the blank with the past perfect continuous form of the verb in parentheses.

1. Because of the smell, I could tell that someone _____ *had been baking* _____ a cake. (bake)

2. When we arrived, she was studying, but she _____ TV. (watch)

3. I _____ in Kyoto for ten years when I moved to Tokyo. (live)

4. When the police stopped the car, they told the driver he _____. (speed)

5. I knew that she _____ because her hair was still wet. (swim)

6. He said that he had a tan because he _____ in the sun. (lie)

7. He finally collapsed because he _____ twelve-hour days for weeks. (work)

8. Nobody thought the elevator was dangerous because they _____ up and down in it safely for years. (go)

9. The car _____ well for months before the accident. (run)

10. Alice won the tennis match, although she _____ more golf than tennis. (play)

11. By the time I finished my shopping, I _____ for three hours. (walk)

12. It was clear from his appearance that he _____ well for quite a while. (not sleep)

FUTURE PERFECT TENSE

The future perfect tense describes an action that will take place before another action or time in the future. Form the future perfect tense by placing *will ('ll) have* before the past participle of the verb.

I will (I'll) have gone.	We will (We'll) have gone.
You will (You'll) have gone.	You will (You'll) have gone.
He will (He'll) have gone.	They will (They'll) have gone.
She will (She'll) have gone.	
It will have gone.	

Fill in the blank with the future perfect form of the verb in parentheses.

1. When you arrive, they _____ *will have left* _____. (leave)

2. By August, the flowers _____. (die)

3. If you come at noon tomorrow, I _____ the work. (finish)

4. If she gets here at six o'clock, they _____. (leave)

5. By the time he gets here, they _____ to bed. (go)

6. We _____ this book by June. (finish)

7. I _____ in this country two years next June. (be)

8. By tomorrow, I _____ all these rules. (forget)

9. By the time she finishes college, she _____ many things. (learn)

10. You _____ all about it by this time next year. (forget)

11. Before he leaves, he _____ every show in town. (see)

12. She _____ by two o'clock. (arrive)

13. By the time we get there, they _____ the lesson. (finish)

14. All the trees _____ their leaves by winter. (lost)

15. By the time Carlos leaves New York, he _____ many interesting things. (do)

16. I am sure they _____ the new road by January. (complete)

17. She says that before she leaves, she _____ at every restaurant in town. (eat)

18. All the leaves _____ color by fall. (change)

Fill in the blank with the correct tense of the verb in parentheses.

1. Andy _____*comes*_____ to class on time. (come)

2. Kathy _____ us now. (teach)

3. I _____ in my garden when you called me yesterday. (work)

4. We _____ our exams next week. (have)

5. I _____ to work on the bus this morning. (come)

6. As I _____ to work this morning, I _____ a man who _____ me for directions. (come, meet, ask)

7. I _____ to Yankee Stadium several times. (be)

8. Listen! I think someone _____ the piano. (play)

9. Paula said that she _____ that movie previously. (see)

10. I _____ that novel three or four times. (read)

11. By this time next year, we _____ all the courses. (complete)

12. Your telegram _____ just as I _____ my house. (come, leave)

13. The sun _____ brightly when I got up this morning. (shine)

14. Our class _____ every morning at 8:30. (begin)

15. Occasionally, we _____ to the movies on Sunday. (go)

16. Jorge _____ English for two years. (study)

17. Alma _____ French for a few months last year. (study)

18. My brother _____ to visit me next week. (come)

19. When you telephoned me, I _____ my lesson. (study)

20. Sue _____ from her seat the minute the bell rang. (jump)

21. When we got home, we discovered that Rose _____ and _____ a message on our machine. (call, leave)

22. Mr. Smith _____ as he _____ the street. (fall, cross)

NEGATIVE FORM

Review

Change the statement to the negative form. Use contractions whenever possible.

1. She speaks English well.

   She doesn't speak English well.

2. We went to the movies last night.

   _____

3. You should tell him.

   _____

4. He should go there soon.

   _____

5. I have lived there for many years.

   _____

6. They were supposed to leave yesterday.

   _____

7. She can speak French perfectly.

   _____

8. The mechanic will be back by eight o'clock.

   _____

9. He had to work late last night.

   _____

10. My friend lives in Los Angeles.

    _____

11. She is the best student in our class.

    _____

12. You may park here.

    _____

13. There were many students absent from class yesterday.

    _____

14. They were driving very fast at the time.

    _____

Change the statement to the question form.

1. They should go home.

   Should they go home?

2. Mr. Ralston can speak Chinese fluently.

   _____

3. She should spend more time at home.

   _____

4. He may sit in this chair.

   _____

5. They can meet us in Los Angeles.

   _____

6. Her brother-in-law can't drive.

   _____

7. Ruth should eat less candy.

   _____

8. You should tell her the truth.

   _____

9. We should speak to her about it.

   _____

10. They may leave now.

    _____

11. The entire tour group can go by van.

    _____

12. You should send them an e-mail message.

    _____

13. He should work at home.

    _____

14. They may wait in the office.

    _____

Review 2

Change the statement to the question form using the question words in parentheses.

1. They live in a nice house. (Where)

   Where do they live?

2. There are a lot of students in this class. (How many)

   _____

3. She may wait for the doctor. (Where)

   _____

4. The plane arrived late. (What time)

   _____

5. It is early now. (What time)

   _____

6. He went to Chicago. (How)

   _____

7. She should leave early. (What time)

   _____

8. They are in Bill's office right now. (Where)

   _____

9. The book cost a lot. (How much)

   _____

10. They work in a different city now. (Where)

    _____

11. Her supervisor lived in Tokyo for quite a while. (How long)

    _____

12. He got up very early this morning. (What time)

    _____

13. They sat in the park for a long time. (How long)

    _____

14. She understands English. (How well)

    _____

Contractions are used a great deal in everyday spoken English. Study them, and try to use them in a natural way.

Fill in the blank with the contracted form of the words in parentheses.

1. _____*He's*_____ a good student. (he is)

2. _____ waiting for us. (they are)

3. _____ be back before noon. (I will)

4. _____ lost my keys. (I have)

5. _____ rent a car in Santo Domingo. (we will)

6. _____ surely finish the work today. (she will)

7. _____ old friends. (we are)

8. _____ planning to leave next week. (they are)

9. _____ almost three o'clock. (it is)

10. Answer the phone. _____ ringing. (it is)

11. _____ just left. (they have)

12. We'll miss the train! _____ leaving the station. (it is)

13. _____ someone at the door. (there is)

14. _____ going to stay in Jamaica all winter. (she is)

15. _____ a big boy for his age. (he is)

16. _____ very kind to say that. (you are)

17. _____ glad that you were able to come. (I am)

18. _____ nothing we can do about it now. (there is)

19. _____ come back when they can. (they will)

20. _____ beginning to snow hard. (it is)

21. _____ need a winter coat in Vermont. (you will)

22. _____ seen the movie before, so I stayed home. (I had)

23. _____ never been to my new apartment. (they have)

24. _____ buy a new car if I won the lottery. (I would)

25. _____ be back in a few minutes. (she will)

26. _____ going to fix the roof as soon as it stops raining. (he is)

SHORT ANSWERS

Write affirmative and negative short answers to the question. Answer you *questions with* I *and* I *questions with* you.

1. Can you speak French?

   a. *Yes, I can.*   b. *No, I can't.*

2. Does she live in San Francisco?

   a. _____ b. _____

3. Have you been sick?

   a. _____ b. _____

4. Is the lesson over?

   a. _____ b. _____

5. Will the Kollers be there, too?

   a. _____ b. _____

6. Are they going out?

   a. _____ b. _____

7. Did she study?

   a. _____ b. _____

8. Was the room warm?

   a. _____ b. _____

9. Is it raining now?

   a. _____ b. _____

10. Should we go home?

    a. _____ b. _____

11. May I use the telephone?

    a. _____ b. _____

12. Can your cousin Tim drive a truck?

    a. _____ b. _____

13. Did it rain yesterday?

    a. _____ b. _____

A tag question is added to the end of a statement. If the sentence is affirmative, the tag question is negative.

> He can speak English, *can't he?*
>
> This bus goes downtown, *doesn't it?*

If the sentence is negative, the tag question is affirmative.

> He can't speak English, *can he?*
>
> This bus doesn't go downtown, *does it?*

Tag questions are usually added to confirm information already known by the speaker.

Fill in the blank with a tag question.

1. He was in Italy, _____ *wasn't he* _____?
2. Claire speaks fluent Spanish, _____?
3. That chair wasn't broken yesterday, _____?
4. It hasn't stopped raining for a week, _____?
5. My car is getting old, _____?
6. You are very good at languages, _____?
7. There'll be enough ice cream for everyone, _____?
8. Sophie seemed pleased with the results of our exams, _____?
9. It has been a very hot day, _____?
10. You won't see him again until next month, _____?
11. He always gets up early, _____?
12. You didn't get to bed very early last night, _____?
13. She can't dance as well as her sister, _____?
14. They dance well together, _____?
15. You are going with us to the movie, _____?
16. You know Ana's brother Sandro, _____?
17. Beds aren't very expensive, _____?
18. He couldn't understand a single word I said, _____?
19. I paid you, _____?
20. The plant hasn't died, _____?

INFINITIVES

Continuous and Perfect Forms

Form the continuous infinitive by placing *to be* before the present participle of the verb. The continuous infinitive describes an action occurring at the time of the main verb of the sentence.

> He seems *to be making* good progress.
>
> She seems too old *to be doing* that work.

Form the perfect infinitive by placing *to have* before the past participle of the verb. The perfect infinitive describes an action that occurred at a time earlier than that of the main verb of the sentence.

> I am sorry *to have made* such a mistake.
>
> I am glad *to have met* you.

A. *Fill in the blank with the continuous infinitive form of the verb in parentheses.*

1. She seems _____ *to be finding* _____ her work easy. (find)

2. He appears _____ his classes. (enjoy)

3. I have _____ something every minute. (do)

4. You ought _____ more time on your English. (spend)

5. Vincent appears _____ his best. (try)

6. They ought _____ faster. (learn)

7. He is supposed _____ in the next room. (work)

8. She seems _____ trouble with that problem. (have)

B. *Fill in the blank with the perfect infinitive form of the verb in parentheses.*

1. They were supposed _____ *to have come* _____ home early. (come)

2. I am pleased _____ you. (meet)

3. He is supposed _____ already. (arrive)

4. My boyfriend seems _____ himself very much. (enjoy)

5. I am sorry not _____ this matter better. (understand)

6. They are certainly glad _____ that train. (catch)

7. Scott is sorry _____ practice today. (miss)

8. The output of the plant is said _____ a million tons a year. (be)

When it is necessary to indicate a second action after the verbs *make, let, hear, see, watch,* and *feel,* use the simple form of the second verb rather than the infinitive.

> He made us wait a long time.
>
> She let us go home early.
>
> No one saw him leave.

After the verb *help,* either the infinitive or the simple form may be used.

> He helped me to move the chairs.
>
> He helped me move the chairs.

Fill in the blank with either the infinitive or simple form of the verb in parentheses.

1. The teacher let us _____leave_____ early. (leave)

2. The doctor made us _____ three hours. (wait)

3. I need _____ him the money. (give)

4. Will you help me _____ for the book? (look)

5. They wouldn't let me _____ in. (come)

6. We prefer _____ in the morning. (leave)

7. Did you hear him _____ ? (leave)

8. No one saw her _____. (fall)

9. How long did he make you _____? (wait)

10. Don't let him _____ those things. (touch)

11. The nurse made us _____ the medicine. (take)

12. She seems _____ that we are going. (know)

13. Have you heard him _____ the piano? (play)

14. He helped me _____ the book. (write)

15. Everyone heard them _____. (laugh)

16. David appears _____ upset. (be)

17. I watched him _____ the game. (play)

Form the passive voice with *to be* and the past participle of the main verb. The passive voice can be used in all verb tenses.

Active Voice	*Passive Voice*
She brings the mail.	The mail is brought (by her).
She brought the mail.	The mail was brought.
She will bring the mail.	The mail will be brought.
She has brought the mail.	The mail has been brought.

Change the statement from the active voice to the passive voice. Use a by *phrase only in numbers 2, 9, and 10.*

1. They educated him in Europe.

   He was educated in Europe.

2. He carried the heavy box.

   _____

3. The people recognized the president immediately.

   _____

4. Someone has stolen my umbrella.

   _____

5. They will deliver the merchandise in the morning.

   _____

6. Ms. Davis had already finished the portrait.

   _____

7. They finished the work in time.

   _____

8. We heard the cries of wolves in the distance.

   _____

9. The rangers found a young tiger in the open field.

   _____

10. The rangers' truck frightened the tiger.

    _____

When a verb in the active voice has both a direct and an indirect object, the indirect object can become the subject when the sentence is changed to the passive form.

Active Voice	Passive Voice
They gave *him* a hundred dollars.	*He* was given a hundred dollars.
They told *us* exactly where to sit.	*We* were told exactly where to sit.

Change the sentence to the passive voice. Make the indirect object the subject of the new sentence. Do not use a by *phrase.*

1. She told me the story.

   I was told the story.

2. They taught us two languages.

   _____

3. She sent us an invitation.

   _____

4. The police gave the man a reward of a hundred dollars.

   _____

5. Our committee will send her flowers.

   _____

6. The guide showed us the principal spots of interest.

   _____

7. A friend told me the news last night.

   _____

8. We have asked everyone the same question.

   _____

9. Someone gave the information to the police.

   _____

10. Our boss has promised each of us a raise.

   _____

Continuous Form

Form the passive voice of the continuous tenses with the continuous form of *to be* and the past participle of the main verb.

Active Voice	Passive Voice
He is writing the letter.	The letter is being written.
She was fixing the car.	The car was being fixed.

Change the statement from the active voice to the passive voice. Do not use a by *phrase.*

1. They are putting the car away.

   The car is being put away.

2. The organization was sending him to school.

   _____

3. We are arguing the case now.

   _____

4. They are building a new subway in that city.

   _____

5. He is putting some chairs in that room now, isn't he?

   _____

6. They are faxing a letter now, aren't they?

   _____

7. They are tearing down the building across the street.

   _____

8. The gardener is watering the plants.

   _____

9. The jury is discussing the verdict now.

   _____

10. They were constructing many new buildings in Caracas when I was there.

    _____

11. They are keeping the streets much cleaner now.

    _____

With modal auxiliaries and related expressions like *can, may, must, have to, ought to,* and *should,* form the passive voice with *be* and the past participle of the main verb.

Active Voice	*Passive Voice*
He can send the box.	The box can be sent.
She has to move her car.	Her car has to be moved.

Change the statement to the passive voice. Do not use a by *phrase.*

1. We must finish those letters.

   Those letters must be finished.

2. They should take the box to Philadelphia.

   _____

3. We have to start the engine first.

   _____

4. We may organize a new group.

   _____

5. I ought to cancel my appointment.

   _____

6. They cannot hold the meeting in that room.

   _____

7. The store may deliver the computer while you're out.

   _____

8. Sheila has to pay her credit card by the first of the month.

   _____

9. She must pay the other bills by the end of the month.

   _____

10. You ought to water the plants once a week.

    _____

Negative Form

Form negatives with the passive voice by placing *not* after the correct form of *to be*.

> **The class is not taught by Mr. Molina.**
>
> **The thief was not caught by the police.**

When an auxiliary such as *will, have,* or *can* is used, *not* always follows the auxiliary.

> **The computer will not be delivered until tomorrow.**
>
> **The ship had not been sunk by the enemy.**

Change the statement to the negative form.

1. The book was published.

   The book was not published.

2. My history teacher was born in Philadelphia.

   _____

3. The garden was watered.

   _____

4. The mail is delivered at ten o'clock.

   _____

5. His car was stolen from in front of his house.

   _____

6. The goods will be delivered on Wednesday.

   _____

7. The thief was sent to prison.

   _____

8. This door can be opened with this key.

   _____

9. The children were put to bed.

   _____

10. The new cell phones will be delivered tomorrow.

    _____

11. The table has been moved.

    _____

Form questions in the passive voice by placing *to be* or an auxiliary verb before the subject.

> **Is the dog fed in the evening?**
>
> **Were the windows washed last week?**
>
> **Will the sofa be delivered by tomorrow?**
>
> **Should the checks be signed right now?**

Change the statement to the question form.

1. The rooms in this hotel are cleaned every day.

   Are the rooms in this hotel cleaned every day?

2. The music can be heard in the next room.

   _____

3. This company is owned by its employees.

   _____

4. This class is taught by Professor Parks.

   _____

5. The house should be painted soon.

   _____

6. Dr. Schmidt will be assisted by Dr. Fleurat.

   _____

7. The stores will be closed early tomorrow.

   _____

8. The electricity has been turned off.

   _____

9. Both doors were opened with the superintendent's key.

   _____

10. He was very much discouraged by his failures.

    _____

11. They were surprised by his behavior.

    _____

12. Her arm was broken in three places.

    _____

If the main verb of a sentence is in the past tense, put the verbs of the dependent clause in the past or past perfect tense.

> Andrew *said* he *knew* Jessica very well.
>
> Andrew *said* he *had known* Jessica very well.

Under this rule, the modal auxiliaries *can, may,* and *will* change to their respective past tense forms *could, might,* and *would* when they are part of the dependent clause.

> Josh *said* that he *could swim* well.
>
> Lynn *said* that she *would be* there by noon.

Choose the correct form of the verb in parentheses.

1. He said he _____would_____ be here. (will, would)

2. She says she _____ come back later. (may, might)

3. She thinks she _____ do it. (can, could)

4. I asked him whether we _____ buy the tickets in advance. (can, could)

5. Tom asked them whether they _____ coffee or tea. (prefer, preferred)

6. He said that he _____ wait for us in the lounge. (will, would)

7. I didn't know what the word _____. (means, meant)

8. Our lawyer says she _____ a lot of work to do. (has, had)

9. The newspaper says it _____ rain tomorrow. (will, would)

10. He told me that they _____ a field at the time. (are crossing, were crossing)

11. Laura said she _____ away tomorrow. (is going, was going)

12. She said she _____ be here in a short time. (will, would)

13. I think he _____ twenty-five years old. (is, was)

14. I thought he _____ a good friend of mine. (is, was)

15. Mr. Chung says he _____ feel well. (doesn't, didn't)

16. She said her work _____ her busy. (keeps, kept)

17. The gardener said the flowers _____. (have died, had died)

18. Her mother gave her the dress she _____. (wants, wanted)

19. She said her mother _____ a bad memory. (has, had)

20. Her mother said she always _____ the important things. (remembers, remembered)

Examine the two sentences carefully:

> Eric said, "I am going away on Wednesday."
>
> Eric said that he was going away on Wednesday.

The first sentence is an example of direct speech because the words of the speaker are given exactly as spoken. The second sentence is an example of indirect speech because the words of the speaker are not given as spoken but are reported.

Note that when changing from direct to indirect speech, we change all the pronouns to agree with the sense of the new sentence. For example, the pronoun *I* in the first sentence was changed in the second sentence to *he*. Note also that in indirect speech, if the reporting verb is in the past tense, the rule of sequence of tenses must be followed. For example, *am going* was changed to *was going* in the second sentence.

Change the sentence from direct to indirect speech.

1. The doctor said, "Kenji is sick."

   The doctor said that Kenji was sick.

2. Nick said, "It is getting late."

   _____

3. He said, "We will have to hurry."

   _____

4. Watson said, "It looks like rain."

   _____

5. Monique said, "I have seen that movie."

   _____

6. Sue said, "I can leave them a message."

   _____

7. Mr. Kovacs said, "I have to go to the customs office."

   _____

8. The man said, "I need more time to complete the project."

   _____

INDIRECT SPEECH

Questions

When direct questions are expressed in indirect speech, the question form is not retained. Indirect questions have statement word order.

> **Rob asked where Clara lived.**

If a direct question does not begin with some question word like *when, where,* or *how,* it must be introduced by *if* or *whether* when expressed in the indirect form.

> **Adela asked if Ali lived near the school.**
>
> **Adela asked whether Ali lived near the school.**

Change the sentence to the indirect speech form. Answer you *questions with* I.

1. He said, "Where do you live?"

   He asked where I lived.

2. Ms. Cruz asked, "Do you like New York?"

   _____

3. She asked, "What time is it?"

   _____

4. Melanie asked, "Where is Busch Gardens?"

   _____

5. He asked, "Does Paolo sing well?"

   _____

6. The man asked, "How are you?"

   _____

7. My professor asked, "Where is the meeting?"

   _____

8. She asked, "Why are you late?"

   _____

9. The teacher asked, "Where is Andorra?"

   _____

Orders or commands are expressed in indirect speech by use of an infinitive.

> **Mr. Murphy told me to come back in ten minutes.**
>
> **Angela told him not to wait for the delivery.**

Change the statement to the indirect speech form.

1. She said to me, "Be quiet."

   She told me to be quiet.

2. They said to me, "Don't go."

   _____

3. I said to him, "Leave me alone."

   _____

4. You said to him, "Close the door."

   _____

5. She said to me, "Don't turn off the computer."

   _____

6. Anne said to David, "Drive carefully."

   _____

7. He said to her, "Think it over."

   _____

8. They said to me, "Come back later."

   _____

9. My father said to us, "Don't jump on the bed."

   _____

10. He said to her, "Don't come late."

    _____

11. My doctor said to him, "Take two aspirins and plenty of vitamin C."

    _____

CAUSATIVE FORM

When we wish to show that some action was performed not by ourselves but by somebody else at our instigation, we use the verbs *to have* or *to get* and the past participle of the main verb.

> I *have* my shoes *shined*.
>
> He *got* his car *washed*.

A. *Change the statement to the causative form. Use the correct form of the verb* to have.

1. I often cut my hair.

   I often have my hair cut.

2. Sarah pressed her sweater.

   _____

3. Larry overhauled his old van.

   _____

4. I must fix my printer.

   _____

5. The front office mailed those letters.

   _____

6. We must paint our apartment.

   _____

B. *Change the statement to the causative form. Use the correct form of the verb* to get.

1. The tenant must clean the rugs.

   The tenant must get the rugs cleaned.

2. Ms. Jackson painted her office.

   _____

3. She is going to manicure her nails.

   _____

4. You should repair the roof.

   _____

5. I will fill the water tank.

   _____

6. My mother weeded her rose garden.

   _____

When a noun is the principal word in an exclamatory sentence, begin the sentence with *what*.

What a beautiful day it is!	**What a pretty flower!**

To give emphasis to an adjective or an adverb in an exclamatory sentence, begin the sentence with *how*.

How well he swims!	**How tall she is!**

Change the statement to the exclamatory form by using what *or* how.

1. She plays the piano very well.

   How well she plays the piano!

2. He is very handsome.

   _____

3. Her oldest daughter is a bright young lady.

   _____

4. They have learned English very quickly.

   _____

5. You have a beautiful new car.

   _____

6. Helen drives very well.

   _____

7. Ryan has grown very tall.

   _____

8. Paris is a charming city.

   _____

9. She has good taste.

   _____

10. They have a gorgeous home.

    _____

EMPHATIC FORM

Use *do, does,* and *did* plus the simple form of the verb in affirmative sentences to express emphasis or strong feeling.

> I *do* feel tired. We *did* finish our assignment.

Change the verb in italics to the emphatic form.

1. He *mentioned* it to you.

   He did mention it to you.

2. She thinks he *knows* the song.

   _____

3. Fred didn't come, but he *called.*

   _____

4. I *liked* it very much.

   _____

5. *Come* back later.

   _____

6. *Visit* us again sometime.

   _____

7. She *enjoys* her lessons.

   _____

8. We *did* these exercises.

   _____

9. I don't like movies, but I *like* the theater.

   _____

10. *Tell* us all about it.

    _____

11. He *tried* to please us.

    _____

12. We don't make much money, but we *have* a lot of fun.

    _____

Use *so* after *think, believe, hope,* and *to be afraid* to respond to a question or to comment upon a statement.

Is Mark coming to the party?	I don't think so.
Is she too old for that work?	I believe so.
Sue will be back soon.	I hope so.
Are we going to be late?	I'm afraid so.

Use so *plus the verb in parentheses to answer or comment.*

1. Do we have time to call them? (think)

   I think so.

2. Will Anthony be happy in that job? (not think)

   _____

3. The stores are open today, aren't they? (believe)

   _____

4. Perhaps he will give us the money. (not think)

   _____

5. It was Cortés who conquered Mexico, wasn't it? (believe)

   _____

6. He will probably fail his exam. (be afraid)

   _____

7. Can you finish the report by tomorrow? (believe)

   _____

8. Is it going to be sunny this afternoon? (hope)

   _____

9. Are we going to be late for class? (think)

   _____

10. Is that movie worth seeing? (believe)

    _____

11. Do they speak Spanish in Brazil? (not believe)

    _____

EXPRESSIONS OF AGREEMENT

So, Indeed, Of Course, Naturally

Use *so* with a subject and an auxiliary verb to express surprise or agreeable astonishment.

> Your computer is down. So it is!
>
> The phone just rang. So it did!
>
> The light has gone out. So it has!

Use various other words to express emphatic agreement.

> Betty has made great progress. Indeed she has!
>
> Perhaps they are right. Of course they are!
>
> He'll try to convince you of it. Naturally he will!

There in *there is/are* sentences is treated like a subject in this construction.

Complete the short responses.

1. The window is wide open. So _____ *it is!* _____
2. There is good weather ahead. Indeed _____
3. They have the same point of view. Of course _____
4. Tony must get more rest. Naturally _____
5. Mr. Kim has made good progress so far. Indeed _____
6. She is an excellent cook. Indeed _____
7. That glass is cracked. So _____
8. Anne is in the next room. So _____
9. Perhaps she owns a lot of property. Indeed _____
10. There are plenty of seats left. Of course _____
11. Your coffee is getting cold. So _____
12. This medicine can help you a lot. Of course _____
13. He can understand a great deal of English. Of course _____
14. They'll win first prize easily. Naturally _____
15. It's four o'clock already. So _____
16. Linda and Jim are great kids. Indeed _____
17. I'm doing better work now, don't you agree? Of course _____
18. It's very hot today, isn't it? Indeed _____

Use *too* and *so* with a subject and an auxiliary verb to avoid the repetition of earlier words or phrases in an affirmative sentence.

> She speaks English well, and he speaks English well.
> She speaks English well, and *he does, too.*
> She speaks English well, and *so does he.*
>
> George went there, and Lawrence went there.
> George went there, and *Lawrence did, too.*
> George went there, and *so did Lawrence.*

Fill in the blank with the correct auxiliary verb.

1. Natasha wants to study English, and Boris _____*does*_____, too.
2. You like San Francisco, and so _____ your wife.
3. Maria saw the movie, and so _____ I.
4. She is sick, and you _____, too.
5. I will leave soon, and so _____ you.
6. We heard the explosion, and he _____, too.
7. She has traveled all over the world, and he _____, too.
8. They enjoyed the movie, and we _____, too.
9. Teresa is bright, and so _____ her cousin, Matt.
10. Michiko will leave soon, and so _____ William.
11. I knew what they were doing, and Rita _____, too.
12. Carla is going to study Portuguese, and so _____ her brother.
13. He has been to Europe, and I _____, too.
14. Alice saw the accident, and so _____ I.
15. They are going to be late for class, and so _____ we.
16. They want to give something, and I _____, too.
17. The meat was salty, and the vegetables _____, too.
18. My watch is slow, and so _____ Peter's.
19. He will help us, and Milton _____, too.
20. I play soccer, and so _____ my roommate.

ABBREVIATED CLAUSES

With *Either* and *Neither*

Use *either* and *neither* with a subject and an auxiliary verb to avoid the repetition of earlier words or phrases in a negative sentence.

> He doesn't speak French, and she doesn't speak French.
> He doesn't speak French, and *she doesn't either.*
> He doesn't speak French, and *neither does she.*

A. *Shorten the statement using* either.

1. She doesn't study English, and he doesn't study English.

   She doesn't study English, and he doesn't either.

2. He didn't go, and I didn't go.

   _____

3. He didn't study, and Marc didn't study.

   _____

4. She won't be there, and her sister won't be there.

   _____

5. Dolores hasn't heard the tape, and you haven't heard the tape.

   _____

6. You can't speak Latin, and Desmond can't speak Latin.

   _____

B. *Shorten the statement using* neither.

1. Jane wasn't in class, and her friend wasn't in class.

   Jane wasn't in class, and neither was her friend.

2. Marta doesn't know them, and we don't know them.

   _____

3. Your watch doesn't have the right time, and my watch doesn't have the right time.

   _____

4. She hasn't seen him, and I haven't seen him.

   _____

5. Paula never rests, and Mindy never rests.

   _____

6. He wouldn't say that, and I wouldn't say that.

   _____

Supposed to shows obligation on the part of the subject. The phrase is used only in the present and past tenses.

> They *are supposed* to be here now.   They *were supposed to* be here an hour ago.

Fill in the blank with the correct form of supposed to *and the verb in parentheses.*

1. They _____ *are supposed to leave* _____ at ten o'clock. (leave)

2. Helen _____ here at five o'clock. (come)

3. You _____ the merchandise last week. (deliver)

4. Barry _____ me the book last month. (send)

5. She _____ this letter yesterday. (send)

6. I _____ a composition tonight. (write)

7. Mr. Robinson _____ here now. (be)

8. Everyone _____ that trip. (take)

9. The train _____ faster than the bus. (be)

10. Kathleen _____ here yesterday. (call)

11. Alice _____ a better student than Nan. (be)

12. We _____ a story about Washington in our English class. (read)

13. He _____ me tomorrow. (call)

14. I _____ at school at nine o'clock. (arrive)

15. They _____ me at the concert. (meet)

16. The students _____ at least two hours on their homework. (spend)

17. The company _____ this book last year. (publish)

18. I _____ early every day. (get up)

19. You _____ these chairs in the next room. (put)

20. The cook _____ dinner by eight o'clock. (prepare)

21. The children _____ to bed early tonight. (go)

22. This dictionary _____ the best. (be)

USED TO

Used to describes a past habit or situation that no longer takes place.

> **She used to teach. (She taught for some time in the past, but now she does not teach.)**
>
> **I used to work for that company. (Now I work for another company.)**

Used to is followed by the simple form of the verb.

Change the sentence to the used to *form.*

1. She walked to work.

   She used to walk to work.

2. He worked here.

   _____

3. She came to class on time.

   _____

4. Monica was an industrious student.

   _____

5. He rode the subway to work.

   _____

6. Colette brought me flowers every day.

   _____

7. Mike played the trumpet very well.

   _____

8. He studied hard.

   _____

9. My adviser helped me very much.

   _____

10. I lived on Forty-sixth Street.

    _____

11. Her father went to that college.

    _____

12. I knew her well.

    _____

Students sometimes confuse *used to* with *to be used to. Used to* describes a past habit or situation. *To be used to* means "to be accustomed to." The expression is always followed by a noun or a gerund.

> I *used to* wear glasses. (I wore glasses at one time, but I do not wear them now.)
>
> I *am used to* wearing glasses. (I am accustomed to wearing glasses.)

Fill in the blank with used to *or the correct form of* to be used to.

1. a. She _____*used to*_____ play tennis well.

   b. She _____*is used to*_____ playing tennis with professionals.

2. a. You _____ exercise at night.

   b. You _____ exercising at night.

3. a. Linda _____ wear glasses at all times.

   b. Linda _____ wearing glasses all the time.

4. a. I _____ studying with a voice teacher.

   b. I _____ study with a voice teacher.

5. a. He _____ live in New York.

   b. He _____ living in New York.

6. a. We _____ having our English class early.

   b. We _____ have our English class early.

7. a. Grace _____ work as a gardener.

   b. Grace _____ working as a gardener.

8. a. I _____ have a large breakfast every morning.

   b. I _____ having a large breakfast.

9. a. They _____ go to bed very early.

   b. They _____ going to bed very early.

10. a. He _____ have his hair cut once a week.

    b. He _____ having his hair cut by the same barber.

11. a. Ken _____ studying all night long.

    b. Ken _____ study all night long.

12. a. She _____ clean the house.

    b. She _____ cleaning the house.

HAD BETTER

Had better refers to a present or future action that is necessary or advisable. It is similar in meaning to *should*. *Had better* is followed by the simple form of the verb and is usually contracted with personal pronouns.

> *You'd better* see a doctor.
> *He'd better* study.
> *Tom had better* come early.

Form the negative by placing *not* after *better*.

> *You'd better not* leave now.
> *He'd better not* spend that money.

Change the statement using had better. *Use the contracted form with personal pronouns.*

1. It will be better if you come back later.

   You'd better come back later.

2. It will be better if he sees a doctor.

   _____

3. It will be better if Sue rests for a while.

   _____

4. It is advisable that you take private lessons.

   _____

5. It is advisable that they save a little money.

   _____

6. It will be better if Peter doesn't mention this to anyone.

   _____

7. It is advisable that you eat more fruits and vegetables.

   _____

8. It will be better if she stops seeing him.

   _____

9. It is advisable that Dennis memorize these facts.

   _____

10. It is advisable that your lawyer call my lawyer.

    _____

11. It will be better if we don't give them too many details.

    _____

Would rather indicates present or future preference. It is followed by the simple form of the verb. It is usually contracted with personal pronouns.

> *I'd rather* study in the morning.
>
> *He'd rather* see a movie.

Form the negative by placing *not* after *rather*.

> *I'd rather not* study in the morning.
>
> *He'd rather not listen* to music.

Change the sentence using would rather. *Use the contracted form with personal pronouns.*

1. I prefer to wait outside.

   I'd rather wait outside.

2. She prefers to come back later.

   _____

3. He prefers to watch TV.

   _____

4. They prefer to walk to school.

   _____

5. Dan prefers to do all his homework before he leaves school.

   _____

6. I prefer to stay home tonight and watch TV.

   _____

7. Betty prefers to drive a big car.

   _____

8. We prefer to spend the summer at home instead of in the country.

   _____

9. He prefers not to speak to her about the matter again.

   _____

10. Marie prefers not to mention it to anyone.

    _____

11. She prefers to study in this class.

    _____

Use *should* in the *if* clause of a future possible sentence to give emphasis to the verb or to suggest a possibility that is more remote than that described by the usual present tense verb.

> If Leo should come (i.e., "if by chance Leo comes" or "if it happens that Leo comes"), I will tell him about it.
>
> If it should rain while I am out, please close all the windows.

Notice that *should* is followed by the simple form of the verb.

Put should *in the* if *clause of the statement.*

1. If Ruth happens to call, be sure to notify me.

   If Ruth should call, be sure to notify me.

2. If by chance you pass a mailbox, please mail this letter.

   _____

3. If it happens that the letter arrives, bring it to my office at once.

   _____

4. If by chance Dad hears about it, I won't be able to go.

   _____

5. If you happen to hear the rumor, don't believe it.

   _____

6. If by chance the electricity goes off, we will have to work in the dark.

   _____

7. If the weather happens to turn cold, we will have to cancel the game.

   _____

8. If the dog happens to bite her, she'll probably sue us.

   _____

9. If by chance a police officer happens to see you driving that way, you'll get a ticket.

   _____

10. If you happen to break the glass, you'll have to buy another.

    _____

Raise is a transitive verb. It is always followed by a direct object.

> **George raised the window.**
>
> **Mary raised her hand.**

Rise is an intransitive verb and is never followed by an object.

> **The sun rises at seven o'clock.**
>
> **Joe rose slowly to his feet.**

Set is a transitive verb, like *raise*, and is followed by a direct object. *Sit*, like *rise*, is intransitive.

> **Mary set the book on the table.**
>
> **Arthur always sits at this desk.**

A. *Fill in the blank with the correct form of* raise *or* rise.

1. Will you _____*raise*_____ the curtain?

2. The sun _____ every day at six o'clock.

3. She _____ vegetables in her garden.

4. When the teacher asked the question, Norma _____ her hand.

5. The storm grew stronger, and the waves _____.

6. The dough has already _____.

7. Do you mind if I _____ the window?

8. Al got angry, _____ to his feet, and left the room.

B. *Fill in the blank with the correct form of* set *or* sit.

1. Mother always _____*sits*_____ at the head of the table.

2. Yesterday he _____ at another desk.

3. Please _____ the package on the floor over there.

4. Twelve people can _____ at this table.

5. Please _____ the table with the good china.

6. Daniela picked up the vase and _____ it on the table.

7. He is _____ in that chair now.

8. You can _____ in this seat near me.

DIFFICULT VERBS

Lay, Lie

Lay, like *raise*, is a transitive verb. It is always followed by a direct object. The past form of *lay* is *laid*; the past participle is *laid*.

> She laid the books on the chair.
>
> They will lay the cornerstone tomorrow.

Lie, like *rise*, is an intransitive verb and is never followed by a direct object. The past form of *lie* is *lay*; the past participle is *lain*.

> Your coat is lying on the floor.
>
> He lay down but could not rest.

A. *Fill in the blank with the correct form of* lay *or* lie.

1. Yesterday he _____*lay*_____ in the sun all day.

2. The dog _____ on the kitchen floor for hours yesterday.

3. You can _____ your coat on that chair.

4. The cat has _____ in that position all afternoon.

5. The carpet was _____ yesterday.

6. Your coat is _____ on the chair in the other room.

7. I thought I _____ it on the sofa in this room.

8. _____ on this sofa for a few minutes until you feel stronger.

9. Although he had _____ a cloth on the floor, the floor got stained.

B. *Fill in the blank with the correct form of the verb in parentheses.*

1. Help me _____*raise*_____ the window. (raise, rise)

2. The hot-air balloon _____ silently in the east. (raised, rose)

3. The president _____ at dawn every morning. (raises, rises)

4. You can _____ the lamp on this table. (set, sit)

5. She _____ her coat over the back of the chair. (laid, lay)

6. Do you like to _____ in the sun? (lay, lie)

7. They are going to _____ the wages of their employees. (raise, rise)

8. Prices are _____. (raising, rising)

9. He has been _____ here asleep since two o'clock. (laying, lying)

The present and past participle verb forms can be used as adjectives. The past participle is often used to describe a feeling. The present participle is often used to describe the cause of a feeling.

Past Participle	*Present Participle*
The children are bored in class.	The class is boring.
We were frightened when we saw that movie.	It was a frightening movie.

Choose the correct form of the adjective in parentheses.

1. Last night's snowstorm was _____ surprising _____. (surprised, surprising)

2. We all felt _____ when we saw the snow. (surprised, surprising)

3. I was really _____ when I read that story. (interested, interesting)

4. It was a really _____ story. (interested, interesting)

5. Many people think insects are _____. (disgusted, disgusting)

6. They feel _____ when they see insects. (disgusted, disgusting)

7. Ellen's parents were _____ when they saw her good grades. (pleased, pleasing)

8. The face of an _____ person usually turns bright red. (embarrassed, embarrassing)

9. Mountain climbing can be a very _____ sport. (excited, exciting)

10. If you are _____ in class, you should ask the teacher for help. (confused, confusing)

11. The children seemed _____ by the soft music. (soothed, soothing)

12. I find a morning walk to be very _____. (energized, energizing)

13. Howard explained the answer to me, but his explanation was very _____. (confused, confusing)

14. The _____ fans shouted and waved when the movie star walked by. (excited, exciting)

15. Her mother thinks warm milk is a very _____ drink. (soothed, soothing)

In Modifying Phrases

The present participle (*ing*) form of the verb can be used in phrases that express cause and effect or time relationships.

When he saw her approach, John ran away.	Seeing her approach, John ran away.
Because she works two jobs, Elaine has little free time.	Working two jobs, Elaine has little free time.

Having plus the past participle indicates an action or situation that took place earlier than that of the main verb of the sentence.

Because he studied hard all semester, Sam got an excellent grade on his final exam.	Having studied hard all semester, Sam got an excellent grade on his final exam.
After they had finished their homework, the children went outside to play.	Having finished their homework, the children went outside to play.

Change the clause in italics to a participial construction.

1. *When I arrived there*, I found Frances sick.

   <u>Arriving there, I found Frances sick.</u>

2. *After she had finished the work*, she left.

   _____

3. *When I saw her*, I cried with joy.

   _____

4. *After he had spoken to her*, he was very happy.

   _____

5. *After he had heard her explanation*, he had to forgive her.

   _____

6. *When we were leaving the party*, we ran into Joyce and Tom.

   _____

7. *After they had left here*, they went to another party.

   _____

8. *After she had stayed outside all day without a coat*, Martha became ill.

   _____

9. *Because I am so busy at work these days*, I don't have much time to spend with my friends.

   _____

A gerund is a verb that ends in *ing* and is used as a noun. Certain verbs in English are always followed by gerunds rather than infinitives. Some of these verbs are *enjoy, mind, stop, avoid, consider, appreciate, finish, deny, admit, risk,* and *dislike*.

> **He apparently enjoys *studying* English.**
>
> **Do you mind *closing* the window?**
>
> **He has stopped *taking* English lessons.**

Fill in the blank with the gerund form of the verb in parentheses.

1. I am considering ____*taking*____ a trip to Canada next summer. (take)

2. Ralph enjoys _____ his new car. (drive)

3. Mohammed stopped _____ to his English class. (go)

4. Do you mind _____ a few minutes in the hall? (wait)

5. We are considering _____ a more powerful computer. (buy)

6. Did you enjoy _____ through Canada last summer? (travel)

7. Ask that representative whether she minds _____ back this afternoon. (come)

8. They are considering _____ classes in the evening this semester. (hold)

9. We will appreciate _____ an answer immediately. (receive)

10. They have finished _____ our apartment at last. (paint)

11. My mother was driving too fast and couldn't avoid _____ the other car. (hit)

12. Daniel denied _____ the money. (take)

13. You shouldn't risk _____ out if you have a cold. (go)

14. He admitted _____ the mistake after we questioned him. (make)

15. Ursula denied _____ the vase. (break)

16. Do you mind _____ down the radio? (turn)

17. I dislike _____ away from home for long periods of time. (go)

18. She has finished _____ for the day. (work)

19. You shouldn't risk _____ the roses too early. (plant)

20. They should finish _____ the apartment by eight o'clock. (clean)

Since gerunds are used as nouns, they are used after prepositions in the same way that nouns are used. Do not make the mistake of using an infinitive instead of a gerund after prepositions.

| We are both fond *of swimming*. | He insisted *on going* with us. |

Fill in the blank with a preposition and the gerund form of the verb in parentheses.

1. She is fond _____*of studying*_____ music. (study)

2. We apologized _____ late. (arrive)

3. We are not interested _____ about his trip. (hear)

4. The woman had no excuse _____ to leave. (try)

5. I was afraid _____ my direction. (lose)

6. There was no chance _____ him there. (leave)

7. I thanked him _____ me with the project. (help)

8. He stopped us all _____ the president. (meet)

9. She needs more practice _____ English. (speak)

10. We will talk _____ a trip next summer. (take)

11. My son insisted _____ half the way. (drive)

12. We were looking forward _____ your friend from New York. (meet)

13. Nancy is getting tired _____ with computers. (work)

14. Do you have a good reason _____ class yesterday? (miss)

15. There is little possibility _____ this work today. (finish)

16. He has no intention _____ it to anyone. (mention)

17. There is little chance _____ her today. (see)

18. She has no interest _____ that kind of work. (do)

19. His heart attack prevented him _____ with the work. (continue)

20. Who is responsible _____ the dishes at your house? (wash)

21. You can't really blame her _____ the nicer one. (choose)

22. She seems to take pleasure _____ others. (help)

A gerund can be used as the subject of a sentence. It always takes a singular verb.

> **Eating is not allowed on the bus.**
>
> **Exercising daily improves your health.**

A. *Fill in the blank with the gerund form of the verb in parentheses.*

1. _____Driving_____ in the snow can be very dangerous. (drive)

2. _____ tennis is fun, and it's good for your health, too. (play)

3. _____ and _____ are my hobbies. (paint, draw)

4. _____ makes me tired. (walk)

5. _____ the bus is more relaxing. (take)

6. _____ with you has been interesting. (work)

7. _____ early is difficult for me. (wake up)

8. _____ in a cold climate makes you appreciate the sun. (live)

9. _____ a fire is easy if you have a match. (start)

10. _____ and _____ are good for your health. (swim, jog)

B. *Choose the correct form of the verb in parentheses.*

1. Eating ice cream _____makes_____ you fat. (make, makes)

2. Visiting our cousins _____ fun. (has been, have been)

3. Driving _____ longer than flying. (takes, take)

4. Doing those exercises _____ difficult. (were, was)

5. Practicing English every day _____ to improve your skills. (helps, help)

6. Owning pets _____ a big responsibility. (are, is)

7. Visiting New York _____ exciting but expensive. (has been, have been)

8. Counting telephone poles _____ is one way to pass the time on the bus. (are, is)

9. They say that playing the piano _____ your typing skills. (improves, improve)

10. My mother says that wasting food _____ shameful. (are, is)

Despite and *in spite of* are prepositions and must be followed by nouns or noun equivalents.

> **Dr. Gonzalez came despite the horrible weather.**
>
> **She came in spite of my warning.**

If it is necessary to use a clause (a subject and a verb) after *despite* or *in spite of,* use *the fact that*.

> **Dr. Gonzalez came despite the fact that the weather was bad.**
>
> **She came in spite of the fact that I warned her against it.**

A. *Fill in the blank with* despite.

1. He went for a walk _____ the rain.

2. Alma went out _____ the fact that it was stormy.

3. He studies hard _____ his illness.

4. Betty showed up early _____ her terrible cold.

5. _____ the fact that it was cold, we went to the ball game.

B. *Fill in the blank with* in spite of.

1. She left _____ my warning.

2. _____ his illness, he does all the housework.

3. They failed _____ our good advice.

4. _____ the good advice we gave them, they didn't win the prize.

5. I'm going to stay home _____ the fine weather.

C. *Complete these sentences. Use your own words.*

1. They left despite _____.

2. He studied in spite of _____.

3. She arrived late despite _____.

4. I caught the bus despite the fact that _____.

5. He went out without a hat or coat despite _____.

6. She went to the party despite the fact that _____.

7. She became angry despite _____.

8. She was fired despite the fact that _____.

Because is used to introduce the reason for an action or situation.

> **We ate because we were hungry.**

Although is used to introduce an action or situation that has an unexpected result.

> **We didn't eat although we were hungry.**

Fill in the blank with because *or* although.

1. The baby cried ___*because*___ it was tired.

2. I couldn't sleep _____ the neighbor's dogs barked all night long.

3. I couldn't sleep _____ the neighborhood was very quiet last night.

4. Steve never has enough money _____ he earns a good salary.

5. Wilma invited everyone to a party _____ it was her birthday.

6. Richard bought a new car _____ his old one broke down.

7. Andrea bought a new car _____ her old one is still in good condition.

8. I need some help with these exercises _____ I don't understand them.

9. Sam went to work today _____ he wasn't feeling well.

10. I felt cold _____ I was wearing a warm coat.

11. I need a warm coat _____ the weather is cold.

12. Roberta is earning more money now _____ she got a better job.

13. _____ my phone was out of order, I missed his call.

14. _____ he lives in the apartment next door, he always calls me on the phone.

15. They wanted to see the monster movie _____ it got terrible reviews.

16. Sometimes I like to walk to my office _____ it's quite far from my house.

17. I like to walk to work _____ the exercise is good for me.

18. _____ nobody offered to help, he had to cook the whole meal himself.

19. _____ many people offered to help, he cooked the whole meal himself.

20. My daughter's grades aren't so good _____ she seems to study a lot.

SO . . . THAT, SUCH . . . THAT

So . . . that and *such . . . that* are used to show a cause and effect relationship. *So . . . that* is used with adjectives, adverbs, and the quantifiers *many, much, few,* and *little.*

> The weather was *so cold that* we stayed inside.
>
> They walked *so slowly that* they arrived late.
>
> George spends *so much time at work that* he doesn't have time for fun.
>
> Cindy has *so many friends that* she is never alone.

Such . . . that is used with adjectives followed by nouns. Use *such a/an* before singular nouns and *such* before plural and noncount nouns.

> It was *such a cold day that* we stayed inside.
>
> These are *such comfortable shoes that* I never want to take them off.
>
> It was *such difficult homework that* I couldn't finish it.

Fill in the blank with so, such, *or* such a/an.

1. Yesterday was _____ *so* _____ beautiful that we decided to go to the beach.

2. It was _____ beautiful day that we decided to go to the beach.

3. _____ many people came to the picnic that there wasn't enough food.

4. Caroline felt _____ sick that she didn't go to work.

5. The movie was _____ boring that we left early.

6. It was _____ funny movie that we couldn't stop laughing.

7. We bought _____ expensive car that we couldn't afford a vacation.

8. The car was _____ expensive that we decided not to buy it.

9. That is _____ sad music that I always cry when I hear it.

10. It was _____ spicy food that I couldn't eat it.

11. This book is _____ interesting that I can't put it down.

12. They talked _____ fast that I couldn't understand them.

13. We have _____ little time left that we won't be able to finish this project.

14. You gave me _____ good advice that I will always be grateful

15. It was _____ nice hotel that we decided to return there next year.

16. Larry drove _____ quickly that he arrived half an hour early.

ONE

Use *one* or *ones* to avoid repetition of some earlier word in a sentence. Often in such cases, *one* is used together with an adjective that serves to differentiate the second object from the first. Study these examples:

> This fork is dirty; please bring me a clean *one*.
>
> After looking over the new cars, I decided to keep my old *one* for another year.
>
> Professional videos are much better than amateur *ones*.

Substitute one *or* ones *for the word in italics.*

1. This knife is dull. Do you have a sharp *knife?*

   Do you have a sharp one?

2. The last lesson was difficult, but this *lesson* is easy.

   _____

3. This chair is very comfortable, but that *chair* is not.

   _____

4. They have two black cats and three white *cats*.

   _____

5. You were asking about a black notebook. Is this the *notebook* that you lost?

   _____

6. I like all games, but tennis and basketball are the *games* I like most.

   _____

7. We find that it is more fun to take several short trips than one long *trip*.

   _____

8. There were boats of all sizes in the bay, big *boats* and little *boats*.

   _____

9. We took pictures of everything, but the *pictures* we took of the gardens turned out best.

   _____

10. This computer disk is defective; please give me a new *disk*.

    _____

ADJECTIVE FORM OF NOUNS

Write the adjective form of the noun.

1. athlete _____athletic_____
2. thirst _____
3. fool _____
4. quarrel _____
5. man _____
6. child _____
7. greed _____
8. wire _____
9. talent _____
10. hour _____
11. sun _____
12. cloud _____
13. revolution _____
14. hunger _____
15. day _____
16. peace _____
17. need _____
18. dirt _____
19. culture _____
20. beauty _____

21. death _____
22. flower _____
23. week _____
24. month _____
25. taste _____
26. summer _____
27. winter _____
28. Egypt _____
29. Ireland _____
30. China _____
31. Sweden _____
32. Switzerland _____
33. Turkey _____
34. Spain _____
35. Mexico _____
36. Japan _____
37. Canada _____
38. India _____
39. Greece _____
40. Brazil _____

Write the noun form of the adjective.

1.	sad	*sadness*	21.	desperate
2.	angry		22.	great
3.	deep		23.	beautiful
4.	happy		24.	rough
5.	high		25.	dead
6.	convenient		26.	loud
7.	ugly		27.	selfish
8.	possible		28.	cynical
9.	wide		29.	present
10.	sarcastic		30.	deceitful
11.	absent		31.	bitter
12.	dangerous		32.	sweet
13.	weak		33.	electric
14.	strong		34.	dry
15.	emphatic		35.	hot
16.	silent		36.	bashful
17.	intelligent		37.	proud
18.	generous		38.	dreary
19.	jealous		39.	true
20.	anxious		40.	clear

NOUN FORM OF VERBS

Write the noun form of the verb.

1.	appreciate	*appreciation*		21.	exist	
2.	excite	*excitement*		22.	agree	
3.	depend			23.	improve	
4.	operate			24.	converse	
5.	educate			25.	announce	
6.	act			26.	annoy	
7.	argue			27.	require	
8.	confide			28.	encourage	
9.	create			29.	manage	
10.	imagine			30.	prepare	
11.	reflect			31.	exert	
12.	concentrate			32.	gratify	
13.	enjoy			33.	connect	
14.	discuss			34.	corrupt	
15.	suggest			35.	magnify	
16.	satisfy			36.	settle	
17.	organize			37.	deter	
18.	translate			38.	pay	
19.	motivate			39.	state	
20.	prefer			40.	declare	

Opposites From Prefixes

Many words form their opposites by taking a negative prefix such as *a-*, *dis-*, *im-*, *in-*, *ir-*, *mis-*, *non-*, and *un-*.

Write the opposite of the word listed by adding the necessary prefix.

1. to respect	*to disrespect*	21. dependent	_____
2. visible	*invisible*	22. finished	_____
3. to dress	_____	23. considerate	_____
4. clear	_____	24. to understand	_____
5. regular	_____	25. interesting	_____
6. possible	_____	26. conscious	_____
7. friendly	_____	27. skilled	_____
8. to obey	_____	28. existent	_____
9. to like	_____	29. violence	_____
10. common	_____	30. to please	_____
11. to spell	_____	31. popular	_____
12. fiction	_____	32. sincere	_____
13. typical	_____	33. perfect	_____
14. complete	_____	34. equal	_____
15. probable	_____	35. sensitive	_____
16. to satisfy	_____	36. official	_____
17. to pack	_____	37. to place	_____
18. known	_____	38. to assemble	_____
19. employed	_____	39. comfortable	_____
20. responsible	_____	40. to agree	_____

Suffixes such as *-er, -ian, -ist,* and *-or* can be added to words to mean "a person who does something."

Write the correct word for the definition.

1. A person who teaches   *teacher*
2. A person who plays music   *musician*
3. A person who studies mathematics   _____
4. A person who educates   _____
5. A person who writes   _____
6. A person who makes art   _____
7. A person who writes novels   _____
8. A person who works in journalism   _____
9. A person who bakes   _____
10. A person who gardens   _____
11. A person who works in a library   _____
12. A person who works in politics   _____
13. A person who eats vegetables but no meat   _____
14. A person who paints   _____
15. A person who plays the drums   _____
16. A person who acts   _____
17. A person who skis   _____
18. A person who drives   _____
19. A person who dances   _____
20. A person who studies biology   _____
21. A person who instructs   _____
22. A person who works in a pharmacy   _____
23. A person who plays the piano   _____
24. A person who studies economics   _____

Students sometimes confuse *until* and *as far as*. *Until* is used only with reference to time (*until tomorrow, until next week, until four o' clock*). *As far as* is used with reference to distance, both physical and figurative (*as far as page 10, as far as Seventy-ninth Street, as far as we could go, as far as I am concerned*).

Fill in the blank with until *or* as far as.

1. We waited _____*until*_____ ten o'clock.

2. The tour group walked _____ Rockefeller Center.

3. For tomorrow, study _____ page 76.

4. I have to stay here _____ Michelle calls.

5. We drove _____ Pittsburgh the first day.

6. He plans to stay there _____ February.

7. _____ I am concerned, you can do what you like.

8. I don't have to go to the doctor _____ next week.

9. We went only _____ Exercise D in yesterday's lesson.

10. I guess we won't see you _____ next summer.

11. I won't see you, _____ I can tell, for some time.

12. She walked _____ the stream, then she turned back.

13. My family went _____ Los Angeles on their vacation.

14. Dan will be at the shore _____ late August.

15. The lab won't know _____ the results are in.

16. Astronauts may go _____ Mars in the future.

17. She told me to stay in bed _____ I felt stronger.

18. They went _____ the third lesson, and the bell rang.

19. Don't come in for dinner _____ I call you.

20. Try not to come _____ I have had my shower.

ADVERBS

Of Time and Frequency

While adverbs of time, such as *yesterday, last night,* and *two days ago,* go at the end of the sentence, adverbs of frequency, such as *always, generally, seldom, usually, frequently, never,* and *ever,* go before the main verb.

> He *always* studies with me.   She takes the bus *every day*.

If an auxiliary verb is used, the adverb of frequency goes before the main verb.

> She *has always loved* music.   He *doesn't usually eat* so late.

Adverbs of frequency follow the verb *to be*.

> They *are never* late.   We *were frequently* sick on that trip.

Place the adverb in parentheses in its correct position in the sentence.

1. Rachel reviews the lesson. (never)

   Rachel never reviews the lesson.

2. I saw him on TV. (yesterday)

   _____

3. She comes to meetings on time. (usually)

   _____

4. Luisa prepared her lesson well. (last night)

   _____

5. I watch music videos. (often)

   _____

6. My uncle reads *Time* magazine every week. (generally)

   _____

7. We go for a walk in the park on Sunday. (usually)

   _____

8. My friends and I went for a stroll in the park. (last Sunday)

   _____

9. She takes an early train. (never)

   _____

10. I drink milk. (seldom)

   _____

Still is an indefinite adverb of time meaning "even yet" or "even up to the present." It refers to some continuing action or state. Like adverbs of frequency, *still* precedes the main verb.

> She *is still working* in that office.   They *still live* in the house they were born in.

The negative of *still* is *anymore*. *Anymore* indicates that an action or state has been discontinued. It comes at the end of a sentence.

> She doesn't eat meat *anymore*.   I don't have a car *anymore*.

Fill in the blank with still *or* anymore.

1. Miriam is _____*still*_____ working at the bank.

2. Jimmy doesn't work here _____.

3. They don't live in Miami _____.

4. I am _____ studying English with Ann.

5. We never see you at the school dances _____.

6. She is _____ the best student in the class.

7. I rarely see Carmen _____.

8. He never comes to see us _____.

9. We are _____ good friends, although I don't see them very often _____.

10. My grandmother _____ likes to do her own baking.

11. Do they _____ have that crazy dog that barks at everyone constantly?

12. He doesn't believe they know him _____.

13. He _____ thinks that he knows more English than anyone else.

14. They are _____ angry, but they are not fighting _____.

15. We _____ haven't saved enough money, but we are _____ going to Europe.

16. Ted said he didn't love Joan _____.

17. There are _____ some tickets left for tonight's show.

18. She _____ plays the piano, but she doesn't sing _____.

19. Jack doesn't like school _____, but he _____ goes.

Use *else* to form compounds with words that contain *some, any,* and *no (somebody else, anything else, nowhere else)* as a shorter and more convenient substitute for *some other person, any other thing, no other person,* and so on.

> Did you go *anywhere else* (i.e., any other place) after the dance?
>
> *Nobody else* (i.e., no other person) would believe him.

Else is also compounded with the question words *what, where, how,* and *who* to give the meaning of "other" or "in addition."

> Where *else* did you go?   How *else* could I tell him?
>
> What *else* does she want?   Who *else* came to the party?

Substitute the correct expression with else *for the words in italics. Although* someone else *and* no one else *can be used, use* somebody else *and* nobody else *in this exercise.*

1. Did they go *any other place*?

   Did they go anywhere else?

2. No *other person* helped him with the work.

   _____

3. You must ask *some other person* about it.

   _____

4. *What other person* knows the combination?

   _____

5. They have never sold that merchandise *in any other place*.

   _____

6. Did you see *any other thing* that you liked?

   _____

7. Let's do *some other thing* tonight besides watch TV.

   _____

8. I didn't tell *any other person* about it.

   _____

9. *In what other way* can I paint the room?

   _____

QUESTION WORDS WITH *EVER*

Add *ever* to the words *what, who, where, when,* and *which* to form the compounds *whatever, whoever, wherever, whenever,* and *whichever.* The *ever* adds emphasis to these words and supplies the additional meaning of "regardless of (the situation)" or "no matter what."

> **Whoever** (i.e., anyone who) gets there first will win a prize.
>
> **Wherever** she goes (i.e., regardless of where she goes), everyone likes her.
>
> **Whenever** I go out with him (i.e., no matter when I go out with him), I have a good time.

Fill in the blank with whatever, whoever, wherever, whenever, *or* whichever.

1. We saw flowers _____*wherever*_____ we went.

2. _____ goes to California will find a beautiful climate.

3. He said we could come _____ we wanted.

4. The doctor says he can eat _____ he wants.

5. She said we could bring _____ gift we wanted.

6. I'll go with you _____ you are ready.

7. Sue will be happy with _____ she gets.

8. _____ studies English always has difficulty with the pronunciation.

9. I will follow him _____ he goes.

10. _____ she comes, she always brings us a present.

11. We were free to go _____ we chose.

12. He said, "Come again _____ you like."

13. Hang up your coat _____ you can find a hook for it.

14. You can take _____ one you want, and you can bring it back _____ you wish.

15. I always enjoyed myself _____ I went there.

16. The doctor says Joe can have an appointment _____ he wants.

17. _____ she goes there for lunch, she orders chocolate cake for dessert.

18. _____ has my pen, please return it immediately!

19. _____ she cooks always turns out superb.

EXPRESSIONS OF QUANTITY

Many and *few* are used with plural count nouns. *A lot of* can be used in place of *many*.

Much and *little* are used with noncount nouns, which have no plural form. *A lot of* can be used in place of *much*. In affirmative sentences, only *a lot of* can be used with noncount nouns. *Much* is usually used only in negative sentences and in questions. (See Appendix for a list of common noncount nouns.)

In general, *a lot of* is more commonly used than *much* or *many*.

I don't use *much* sugar.	I need *a lot of* paper.
Do you use *a lot of* sugar?	*Many* people came to my party.
We have *little* money left.	This book has *a lot of* pages.
A lot of rain fell last year.	There are *few* trees on this street.

Fill in the blank with the correct adjective in parentheses.

1. He eats ___*a lot of*___ candy (much, a lot of)

2. There are _____ software companies in that city. (much, many)

3. There isn't _____ honey left in the jar. (many, much)

4. There is _____ grass in that meadow. (many, a lot of)

5. Do you have a _____ extra pencils? (few, little)

6. We had _____ money with us. (few, little)

7. I need a _____ more time to finish. (few, little)

8. She made _____ mistakes. (few, little)

9. We haven't heard _____ news lately. (many, much)

10. A _____ friends are coming over tonight. (few, little)

11. Janie spends too _____ time on her homework. (few, little)

12. There are _____ plants in the hallway. (a lot of, much)

13. How _____ pounds did you lose? (much, many)

14. How _____ weight did you lose? (much, many)

15. We sat there for _____ hours. (much, many)

16. There is _____ snow on the ground. (a lot of, many)

17. There are _____ elegant restaurants in this town. (many, little)

18. There isn't _____ coffee left. (few, much)

19. How _____ languages can you speak? (much, many)

A *few, a little, few,* and *little* all mean "a small amount." *A few* and *a little* convey a positive idea and are similar in meaning to *several* or *some.*

> I have lived here only a short time, but I have already made *a few* friends.
>
> I have *a little* money so I can pay for our movie tickets.

Few and *little* convey a negative idea and are similar in meaning to "not enough" or "almost none."

> I feel very lonely because I have *few* friends.
>
> I can't go to the movies because I have *little* money.

Use *a few* or *a little* after *just* or *only.* Use *few* or *little* after *too* or *very.*

> *Only a few* students are absent today.
>
> I can't go because I have *too little* time.

Fill in the blank with the correct word(s) in parentheses.

1. We need to finish this quickly because we have _____*little*_____ time left. (little, a little)

2. Please put _____ sugar in my coffee because I like it sweet. (little, a little)

3. This is a quiet area because _____ people live here. (few, a few)

4. Jane can't go to the movies with us because she has to do _____ homework. (little, a little)

5. It was a very difficult test, and _____ students passed it. (few, a few)

6. I needed some new winter clothes so I bought _____ sweaters today. (few, a few)

7. _____ friends came by my house last night, and we had dinner together. (Few, A few)

8. I couldn't finish printing the report because the printer had too _____ ink. (little, a little)

9. We need to go to the store because we have only _____ paper left. (little, a little)

10. The trip was canceled because too _____ people wanted to go. (few, a few)

11. I called you _____ times yesterday, but you didn't answer the phone. (few, a few)

12. The lecture wasn't well advertised and _____ people showed up. (few, a few)

13. This region is very dry because _____ rain falls here. (little, a little)

14. Carlos is so thin because he eats very _____ sweets. (few, a few)

Fill in the blank with the correct word(s) in parentheses.

1. He is an old friend of _____*hers*_____. (she, her, hers)

2. I bought this gold pen at _____ store. (Nicks, Nick's)

3. Sheep _____ timid animals. (is, are)

4. Sally sat directly in front of Bill and _____. (I, me)

5. My friends said that _____ could come later. (they, them)

6. Is there _____ money left in your bank account? (much, many)

7. He told Sara and _____ about it. (I, me)

8. The boys will hurt _____ if they are not careful. (himself, themselves)

9. She seemed like _____ thoroughly honest person. (a, an)

10. Mike Lopez is _____ old friend of mine. (a, an)

11. She drove at a speed of eighty miles _____ hour. (a, an)

12. Sam _____ arrives late to class. (every day, always)

13. You can _____ your books on that table. (sit, set)

14. Their trip to China sounds very _____. (exciting, excited)

15. We told Barry and _____ all about it. (they, them)

16. What _____ beautiful day! (a, an)

17. She caught _____ terrible cold last winter. (a, the)

18. Roy is _____ excellent student. (a, an)

19. The technician has already put _____ equipment away. (she, her)

20. The teacher gave _____ his book. (I, me)

21. The children were _____ about going to the circus. (exciting, excited)

22. We _____ are to blame. (ourselves, for ourselves)

23. This book is mine, and that one is _____. (your, yours)

24. My grandparents bought me _____ own car. (my, mine)

In everyday English conversation, avoid beginning any direct question with a preposition. Instead, begin the question with the object of the preposition and shift the preposition to the end of the sentence.

> **What is he looking *for*?**
>
> **What state does she come *from*?**

Supply the correct preposition to complete the question.

1. What are they talking _____*about*_____?

2. What are you thinking _____?

3. What country was he born _____?

4. Whom (who) do you wish to speak _____?

5. What kind of car are you looking _____?

6. Whom (who) does this book belong _____?

7. What are they going to use the money _____?

8. Which restaurant do you want to eat _____?

9. Which dealer did you buy your van _____?

10. Whom (who) was the book written _____?

11. Which hotel did he go _____?

12. Whom (who) did they sell their house _____?

13. Which paintings do you want to look _____?

14. What is the guide pointing _____?

15. Which room do you have your class _____?

16. Where did all this loose change come _____?

17. What are you smiling _____?

18. Whom (who) are you looking _____?

19. Where did you take this book _____?

20. Where do you come _____?

If a sentence contains a relative pronoun that is the object of a preposition, the preposition is generally shifted to the end of the sentence or clause. Notice that in sentences of this type, we frequently drop the relative pronoun altogether.

> **This is the book (that) I was talking about.**
>
> **She is the clerk (that) I spoke to yesterday.**

Change the sentence by dropping the relative pronoun and shifting the preposition.

1. This is the movie about which everyone is talking.

   This is the movie everyone is talking about.

2. The woman to whom you were speaking is my teacher.

   _____

3. That is the store in which I lost my purse.

   _____

4. She is the kind of salesperson from whom it is difficult to get away.

   _____

5. The adviser to whom you should speak is Dr. Kojima.

   _____

6. It is a subject on which we will never agree.

   _____

7. The thing about which they were arguing was really of little importance.

   _____

8. It is a place in which you will feel at home.

   _____

9. It was Charles for whom I had to wait so long.

   _____

10. It was Jack from whom he borrowed the money.

    _____

11. The room in which we study is on the second floor.

    _____

Rob, steal

One steals an object, but one robs a person or thing.

> **They stole money from the bank's safe.**
> **They robbed the bank.**

Some, somewhat

Some is an adjective and must modify a noun or pronoun; *somewhat* is an adverb and is used to modify an adjective or another adverb.

> **He has some money and some food to contribute.**
> **Beatrice feels somewhat better after her trip.**

In, into

In suggests position within a certain space; *into* suggests action toward a certain place.

> **The money is in the drawer.**
> **He threw the money into the drawer.**

Affect, effect, advise, advice

Affect and *advise* are verbs; *effect* and *advice* are nouns.

> **The medicine affected Harold quickly.**
> **He soon felt the effects of the medicine.**
> **She advised me to take the course.**
> **I intend to follow her advice.**

Fill in the blank with the correct word in parentheses.

1. They arrived _____*somewhat*_____ early. (some, somewhat)

2. The _____ of his efforts was obvious. (effect, affect)

3. The _____ of the teacher's discipline were evident. (effects, affects)

4. What do you _____ me to do? (advice, advise)

5. She walked right _____ their trap. (in, into)

6. The thief _____ my watch. (stole, robbed)

7. This coffee seems _____ better than usual. (some, somewhat)

8. The bad news obviously _____ her. (effected, affected)

9. I should have taken your _____. (advise, advice)

Beside, besides
Beside means "alongside of"; *besides* means "in addition to."

> John sits beside me in class.
>
> Two boys besides John took the trip.

Teach, learn
Teach means "to instruct someone else." *Learn* means "to gain knowledge"; it is impossible to "learn" another person.

> Rose taught me how to swim.   I learned French in high school.

Negative openings
Note that if an English sentence begins with a negative word, an auxiliary verb or some form of *to be* must precede the subject, as in interrogative sentences.

> *Never have* I heard such music.   *Not once did* he mention your name.

Fill in the blank with the correct word in parentheses.

1. Two other children _____*besides*_____ Mary left for camp. (beside, besides)

2. Who _____ you how to speak English? (taught, learned)

3. Never _____ seen him so happy. (I have, have I)

4. I put my homework on the seat _____ me. (beside, besides)

5. Melanie is going to _____ us how to knit. (learn, teach)

6. She sits _____ me in class. (beside, besides)

7. He was _____ French by a good teacher. (taught, learned)

8. No one _____ Susanne will have to repeat the class. (beside, besides)

9. Not once _____ taxes. (he mentioned, did he mention)

10. I _____ a lot from Professor Rothman. (taught, learned)

11. Nowhere _____ find a more generous person. (you could, could you)

12. Never _____ happier than when I worked here. (he was, was he)

13. Never have we _____ such a sight! (see, seen)

14. Our teacher _____ about the change in the schedule first. (taught, learned)

No, not

No is an adjective and is used to modify nouns.

> **He has no money and no friends.**

Not is an adverb and is used

    a. to modify verbs
    b. before the adjectives *much, many, any, enough*
    c. before any article or numeral used to modify a noun

> **He does not speak English well.**
>
> **Not many people came to the meeting.**
>
> **Not a person spoke; not one word of protest was heard.**

Spill, pour

Spill suggests some unintentional or accidental action; *pour,* some intentional action.

> **She carelessly spilled the milk on the floor.**
>
> **Joan carefully poured the tea into the cup.**

Win, beat

One wins a game, but one beats or defeats an opponent.

> **Alice won the game of chess easily.**
>
> **Alice easily beat Roger at chess.**

Fill in the blank with the correct word in parentheses.

1. Ben _____*beat*_____ me in a game of poker. (won, beat)

2. There are _____ boys in that class. (no, not)

3. He _____ the game of chess. (won, beat)

4. There are _____ many flowers in that vase. (no, not)

5. The baby _____ cereal all over the floor. (spilled, poured)

6. She _____ the milk into the glass. (spilled, poured)

7. _____ one girl wanted to dance with him. (No, Not)

8. Dennis carefully _____ the cream into the pitcher. (spilled, poured)

9. Who _____ the baseball game? (won, beat)

Fill in articles where needed. If no article is needed, leave a blank.

1. ___The___ chair on which you are sitting is not comfortable.

2. _____ fire which destroyed _____ building started on _____ tenth floor.

3. I bought _____ new hat yesterday. It has _____ wide brim and _____ narrow band. _____ man who sold it to me said it was _____ new style from _____ Paris.

4. The man took _____ his book and put it into _____ his briefcase.

5. They enjoyed _____ speech given by _____ Dr. Lao, who spoke on _____ situation in Vietnam.

6. We all had _____ good time at _____ dance last night.

7. _____ price of _____ gold is rising, but _____ price of _____ silver is falling.

8. Much of _____ silver which we use in _____ United States comes from _____ Montana.

9. _____ drinking water often varies in taste, according to locality. _____ drinking water in New York City is quite good.

10. There are _____ several new magazines on _____ table in _____ hall.

11. We often go to _____ Central Park and watch _____ animals in _____ zoo.

12. Please open _____ windows. _____ air in this room is no good.

13. They plan to visit _____ Russia this summer. I understand _____ Russian language is difficult to learn.

14. Mr. and Mrs. Nomura are now traveling in _____ South America. They plan to visit _____ Venezuela, _____ Colombia, _____ Peru, and _____ Argentina.

15. They will arrive in _____ Netherlands at _____ noon.

16. _____ noon train from _____ Washington comes in on _____ track 10.

17. _____ weather today is very warm.

18. _____ early morning light comes through _____ my window and wakes me up.

19. In _____ cold weather, I always keep _____ window in my room closed.

20. There are more _____ white keys on a piano than there are _____ black keys. I like to use _____ black keys when I play _____ piano because I think those notes make _____ music more interesting.

21. Her boss bought his wife _____ diamond necklace for _____ their anniversary. The year before, he bought her _____ emerald ring.

22. Is it true that _____ South Africa is _____ leading producer of diamonds in _____ world?

Use the comma to separate words, phrases, or clauses in a series.

> **We need books, pencils, chairs, and desks.**
>
> **We played tennis, took long walks, and went swimming.**

Use the comma to set off items in dates, addresses, and geographical names.

> **He lives in Chicago, Illinois.**
>
> **It happened on Tuesday, November 27, 1981.**

Use the comma to set off parenthetical expressions and words in direct address. Also use the comma to set off all appositives.

> **He was, to be sure, an excellent diplomat.**
>
> **And so, my friends, you can see the results.**
>
> **Jack, our butcher, was hurt recently.**

Punctuate the sentences.

1. We study history mathematics geography and reading.

2. Sue Bielski the mechanic repaired our car and also fixed our refrigerator.

3. Mike Madison the head of the company will see you on Sunday.

4. The governor in the first place did not want the action.

5. He was born in Scranton Pennsylvania on March 23 1980 and he has lived there ever since.

6. We cannot after all live forever.

7. By the way do you remember Mrs. Jackson's telephone number?

8. Sue Brown Henry's cousin is visiting him in New York.

9. Where were you Miss Lyons on the morning of June 26 2003?

10. The old Amos Building a famous landmark of the town was recently torn down. As a matter of fact it was torn down on February 12 Lincoln's Birthday.

11. The most popular summer sports are tennis swimming and hiking.

12. Yesterday I met my schoolmates Tom Beck Ruth Sanchez and Randy Owens.

13. The last time I saw them was on August 3 2003.

Commas 2

Use the comma to set off any long adverbial clause that precedes a main clause. Also set off any such clause that occurs out of its normal position and thus interrupts the normal order of the sentence.

> When the wind began to blow hard, we ran for shelter.
>
> We might, if the rain continues much longer, have to postpone our trip.
>
> but
>
> We might have to postpone our trip if the rain continues much longer.

Punctuate the sentences.

1. If it rains we may have to postpone our trip.

2. I may if the weather is bad cancel the class trip.

3. We may have to postpone our trip if it rains.

4. When he protested so vigorously we withdrew our proposal.

5. Because he was so widely read he had a comprehensive grasp of the issues.

6. As soon as we had closed the shop we went home.

7. Because he had been ill he asked to be excused from all assignments.

8. If Monica wanted she could be a very good student.

9. After Yoshiko got her visa she bought an airline ticket.

10. He never studied any foreign language when he was in high school.

11. When he was in high school he never studied any foreign language.

12. He never when he was in high school studied any foreign language.

13. Although she was a skilled engineer she did not know anything about road building.

14. Natasha as was easily seen from her speech was a woman of strong opinions.

15. He took the kettle an antique he had bought in England off the stove.

16. When the last guest had gone we looked at the pile of dirty dishes sighed and got to work.

17. If you stopped making excuses and just did the work you would be finished in no time.

Use the comma to set off any nonrestrictive clause. A nonrestrictive clause is one that is not necessary to the meaning or identification of the word which it modifies. It is, in other words, a clause that could actually be set off in parentheses.

Use no punctuation at all with restrictive clauses.

> **Nonrestrictive: Dr. Matany,** *who is very skillful*, **has a big practice.**
>
> **Restrictive: Any doctor** *who is very skillful* **has a big practice.**
>
> **Nonrestrictive: Whittier,** *where we met*, **was a pretty little town.**
>
> **Restrictive: The place** *where we met* **was a pretty little town.**

Punctuate the sentences.

1. Barbara who is quite smart deserves to pass.

2. Any student who is lazy does not deserve to pass.

3. Any girl who has good acting ability can audition for the part of the heroine.

4. Angela who has good acting ability was selected for the part of the heroine.

5. Daniel's hands feet and face which were covered with mud were washed by Mother.

6. Any passenger who enters the engine room does so at his or her own risk.

7. The person who said that was mistaken.

8. Eva who told the story was obviously misinformed.

9. Wednesday when my brother is usually out of town will be a good day to call.

10. Ms. Rubio who was in the real estate business decided to promote Glen Acres which was formerly a swamp.

11. The fellow who was laughing was clearly the perpetrator of the joke.

12. His great love for nature which he acquired during his childhood showed itself in his curiosity about any bird flying through his garden.

13. The profit which you can expect on so cheap an article is very small.

14. We heard a noise that resembled the cry of an injured animal.

15. The George Washington Bridge which spans the Hudson River has been very successful financially.

16. Kyle unlike his brother Josh has brown hair blue eyes and a light complexion.

Commas and Semicolons

Use a comma to separate two independent clauses joined by *or, and,* or *but* unless the clauses are very short.

> **In the North there are many wheat fields, but in the South cotton fields predominate.**
>
> **We had great trouble in reaching him, but at last he answered.**

If such clauses are not connected by *or, and,* or *but* yet are related in meaning, they can be joined by a semicolon.

> **In the North there are many wheat fields; in the South cotton fields predominate.**
>
> **We had great trouble in reaching him; at last, however, he answered.**

Punctuate the sentences.

1. Chicago is my favorite city but Philadelphia offers more advantages.
2. Fools need advice only wise men profit by it.
3. The general manager will talk to you soon and will give you the information.
4. Alec is a very good automobile mechanic and his prices are low.
5. I had the jacket for a week but then finally I returned it.
6. She kept the book for a long time but she finally returned it.
7. Bill had the ring then he gave it to Joe.
8. Marcia didn't go but Colleen did.
9. Mary was highly pleased with the results therefore she showed her pleasure and gave us all a day off.
10. Lou was pleased with the results but Mr. Martin obviously wasn't.
11. Cowards die many times but a brave man dies only once.
12. Marianne was cautious but Henry bet on the black horse and won more than a hundred dollars.
13. Tom plays the bass and Dennis plays the acoustic guitar.
14. I like board games my sister likes computer games.
15. He was tattered and dirty but he ate like a gentleman.
16. My brother or my mother will help you and will gladly show you the way.

Punctuate the statements.

1. The changes which we are planning will soon be completed.

2. Jenny and Alice came into the room looked around whispered to each other and then walked out.

3. Williams store which sells many fancy groceries was recently repainted and as a consequence it now looks very nice.

4. I am sure Sophie said Henry you will like our new summer place which was built by the local company.

5. Of course Father its a pity said Ellen that people don't appreciate the excellent work that you have done here.

6. We drove from Harrisburg to Albany which is the capital of New York state.

7. Mary and Ellen stopped and watched Henry and Joseph running and jumping.

8. We Mary Ethel and I considered going but later we changed our minds and decided to stay at home and rest.

9. The woman whom we saw yesterday was Don Grays sister Terry Nelson who is a psychologist.

10. Saturday Jan 16 was the coldest day that we had but the next day seemed even colder to me.

11. Everyone got into the van we started out and soon we were on the freeway.

12. At 11:00 Rex adjourned the meeting no decision having been reached by that time.

13. I believe said the visitor that Mr Davis should be notified at once yet we all realize that the duty is not a pleasant one.

14. Strangely enough Heather and Jennifer came into the room looked at the table sat down and began to read.

15. She is very intelligent but the lack of a diploma would prevent her from entering any college even one of low standards.

16. They didn't notice the mail carrier he came by every day at that time.

17. Having never traveled abroad she sought our advice on hotels transportation money exchange and much more besides that.

18. Louise never admitted when she was wrong being unjustifiably sure of her own judgments.

SPELLING RULES

The four simple rules of spelling that follow are very helpful. Try to memorize them.

a. A word ending in silent *e* generally drops the *e* before a suffix beginning with a vowel and retains it before a suffix beginning with a consonant.

move ⟶ movable   like ⟶ likable   move ⟶ movement   like ⟶ likely

After *c* or *g*, if the suffix begins with *a* or *o*, the *e* is retained in order to keep the soft sound of *c* or *g*.

notice ⟶ noticeable   change ⟶ changeable   advantage ⟶ advantageous

b. In words with *ie* or *ei*, use *i* before *e*, except after *c*, when the sound is "ee."

	believe	fierce	receive	conceive	grief	cashier
Exceptions:	neither	either	seize	financier	weird	leisure

c. A noun ending in *y* preceded by a consonant takes the ending *ies* in the plural. A verb ending in *y* preceded by a consonant forms its present tense, third-person singular, with *ies*. If the terminal *y* in such words is preceded by a vowel, then only an *s* is added.

lady ⟶ ladies   valley ⟶ valleys   marry ⟶ marries   enjoy ⟶ enjoys

d. In one-syllable words or words accented on the last syllable that also end in a single consonant and are preceded by a single vowel, double the consonant before a suffix beginning with a vowel.

drop ⟶ dropped   occur ⟶ occurring   offer ⟶ offered   feel ⟶ feeling

---

Practice the spelling of these troublesome words.

adorable	conceivable	excitable	lovable	omitted	shield
armies	conceive	famous	loveless	outrageous	shriek
begging	controlled	feeling	monkeys	permitting	traceable
beginning	daisies	financier	neither	piece	trapped
benefited	deceive	forgetting	noticeable	preferred	turkeys
bingeing	dries	forties	occurrence	priest	usable
canceled	employs	hopeful	occurring	receive	useful
centuries	equipment	incurable	offered	relieve	worshiping
chief	equipped	leisure	offering	seize	

Nouns refer to people, places, things, or ideas. Nouns that are the names of specific people, places, or things are called *proper nouns*. Proper nouns are always capitalized.

Types of proper nouns	Examples of proper nouns
Names of people, including their titles	*George, Ms. Jones, Dr. Einstein*
Names of months, holidays, and days of the week	*December, Independence Day, Tuesday*
Names of places and geographical features	*New York City, Thailand, Maple Street, Andes Mountains*
Names of buildings and monuments	*Empire State Building, Eiffel Tower*
Names of businesses and institutions	*Microsoft Corporation, London School of Economics, United Nations*
Names of languages and nationalities	*Chinese, French, Mexican, Brazilian*
Names of religions	*Buddhism, Christianity, Islam*
Titles of courses*	*Intermediate English, Introduction to Biology*
Titles of movies, TV programs, and publications*	*The Matrix, Grammar to Go, Newsweek*

*In titles, don't capitalize a small word, such as *of* or *the*, unless it is the first word of the title.

Don't confuse proper nouns with common nouns. Proper nouns are specific names; common nouns are not specific names, but are more general terms.

Proper nouns	Common nouns
This car belongs to *Dr. Johnson*.	You should visit the *doctor* when you are sick.
The *Mississippi River* is very long.	I like to go swimming in the *river*.
We plan to visit the *Washington Monument*.	It is a famous *monument*.
I graduated from *Central High School*.	It is a very big *school*.
Sarah is taking *Advanced Mathematics* this semester.	She is very interested in *mathematics*.

Noncount Nouns

Noncount nouns are nouns that don't have a plural form. Often they are things that cannot be counted.

Examples of common noncount nouns

Food	Liquids and gases	Materials
meat	water	metal
flour	milk	gold
sugar	coffee	silver
butter	shampoo	wood
cereal	oil	cotton
fruit	ink	silk
bread	paint	nylon
beef	air	plastic
salt	oxygen	plaster
pepper	steam	clay
soup	smog	glass
Groups of things	**Abstract ideas**	**Weather**
furniture	information	rain
luggage	advice	thunder
jewelry	love	lightning
equipment	beauty	cold
mail	education	heat
money	knowledge	snow
traffic	sadness	ice
vocabulary	anger	fog
	intelligence	wind

Pronouns take the place of nouns.

Subject pronouns are used in the subject position in a sentence.

Sam and Sarah are our neighbors. *They* live next door.

	Singular	Plural
1st person	I	we
2nd person	you	you
3rd person	he, she, it	they

Object pronouns are used in the object position (following a verb or preposition) in a sentence.

Do you like my new shoes? I bought *them* yesterday.

	Singular	Plural
1st person	me	us
2nd person	you	you
3rd person	him, her, it	them

Possessive pronouns take the place of possessive nouns or possessive adjectives plus nouns.

That isn't my coat. *Mine* is in the closet.

	Singular	Plural
1st person	mine	ours
2nd person	yours	yours
3rd person	his, hers, its	theirs

Reflexive pronouns are used when the subject and the object of a sentence refer to the same person or thing.

John cut *himself.*

They are used with the preposition *by* to mean *alone* or *without help*.

Sharon wrote the composition by *herself.*

They are used to emphasize a noun.

Teachers *themselves* sometimes make mistakes.

	Singular	Plural
1st person	myself	ourselves
2nd person	yourself	yourselves
3rd person	himself herself itself	themselves

Spelling Rules for Adding Endings to Words

Adding *s* to nouns to form the plural

most nouns: add *s*	book pencil	books pencils
nouns that end in *s, sh, ch, x, z*: add *es*	dress wish match fox buzz	dresses wishes matches foxes buzzes
nouns that end in a consonant plus *y*: change the *y* to *i* and add *es*	baby city	babies cities
nouns that end in a vowel plus *y*: add *s* only	boy day	boys days
nouns that end in *f* or *fe*: change the *f* or *fe* to *ve* and add *s* (exceptions: belief-beliefs, roof-roofs, chief-chiefs)	leaf wolf life	leaves wolves lives
some nouns that end in a consonant plus *o*: add *es*	tomato hero	tomatoes heroes
nouns that end in a vowel plus *o*: add *s* only	studio	studios

Adding *s* to present tense verbs to form the third-person singular

most verbs: add *s*	walk clean	walks cleans
verbs that end in *s, sh, ch, x, z*: add *es*	pass rush catch fix fizz	passes rushes catches fixes fizzes
verbs that end in a consonant plus *y*: change the *y* to *i* and add *es*	carry study	carries studies
verbs that end in a vowel plus *y*: add *s* only	stay buy	stays buys
(irregular forms: do-does, go-goes, have-has)		

Adding *ing* to verbs for continuous tenses

most verbs: add *ing*	walk clean	walking cleaning
verbs that end in silent *e*: drop the *e* and add *ing*	write dance	writing dancing
verbs that end in a consonant-vowel-consonant pattern in a stressed syllable: double the final consonant before adding *ing*	plan stop begin	planning stopping beginning
verbs that end in a consonant-vowel-consonant pattern in an unstressed syllable: add *ing* only	listen visit	listening visiting
verbs that end in *ie*: change the *ie* to *y* and add *ing*	tie lie	tying lying

Adding *ed* to regular verbs to form the past tense

most verbs: add *ed*	walk clean	walked cleaned
verbs that end in *e*: add *d* only	hope live	hoped lived
verbs that end in a consonant-vowel-consonant pattern in a stressed syllable: double the final consonant before adding *ed*	plan stop permit	planned stopped permitted
verbs that end in a consonant-vowel-consonant pattern in an unstressed syllable: add *ed* only	listen visit	listened visited
verbs that end in a consonant plus *y*: change the *y* to *i* and add *ed*	carry study	carried studied
verbs that end in a vowel plus *y*: add *ed* only	stay enjoy	stayed enjoyed

Adding *er* and *est* to adjectives to form comparatives and superlatives

most one-syllable adjectives: add *er* for the comparative and *est* for the superlative	tall old	taller older	the tallest the oldest
adjectives that end in *e*: add *r* or *st*	safe nice	safer nicer	the safest the nicest
adjectives that end in a consonant-vowel-consonant pattern: double the final consonant and add *er* or *est*	fat hot	fatter hotter	the fattest the hottest
adjectives that end in a consonant plus *y*: change the *y* to *i* and add *er* or *est*	funny easy	funnier easier	the funniest the easiest

Irregular comparative and superlative forms

Adjective	Comparative	Superlative
good	better	the best
bad	worse	the worst
far	farther	the farthest

APPENDIX: GRAMMAR SUMMARY

Verb Tenses

To Be

	Simple Present	Present Continuous	Simple Past	Present Perfect	Past Perfect
I	am	am being	was	have been	had been
you, we, they	are	are being	were	have been	had been
he, she, it	is	is being	was	has been	had been

Present Tenses

	Simple Present	Present Continuous	Present Perfect	Present Perfect Continuous
I	work	am working	have worked	have been working
you, we, they	work	are working	have worked	have been working
he, she, it	works	is working	has worked	has been working

Past Tenses

	Simple Past	Past Continuous	Past Perfect	Past Perfect Continuous
I	worked	was working	had worked	had been working
you, we, they	worked	were working	had worked	had been working
he, she, it	worked	was working	had worked	had been working

Future Tenses

	Simple Future	Future Continuous	Future Perfect
I	will work	will be working	will have worked
you, we, they	will work	will be working	will have worked
he, she, it	will work	will be working	will have worked

The passive voice is formed with the verb *to be* and the past participle form of the verb. The passive voice can be used in all verb tenses.

Tense	Active Voice	Passive Voice
Simple Present	Sam answers the phone.	The phone is answered by Sam.
Present Continuous	Sam is answering the phone.	The phone is being answered by Sam.
Present Perfect	Sam has answered the phone.	The phone has been answered by Sam.
Simple Past	Sam answered the phone.	The phone was answered by Sam.
Past Continuous	Sam was answering the phone.	The phone was being answered by Sam.
Past Perfect	Sam had answered the phone.	The phone had been answered by Sam.
Simple Future	Sam will answer the phone.	The phone will be answered by Sam.

Conditional Sentences

A conditional sentence consists of an *if* clause and a result clause.

- **Future real** conditional sentences use the present tense in the *if* clause and the future tense in the result clause. The modals *can, may*, and *might* are also possible in the result clause.

- **Present unreal** conditionals use the past tense in the *if* clause and *would* plus verb in the result clause. The modals *could* and *might* are also possible in the result clause. The correct form of the verb *to be* in the *if* clause is always *were*.

- **Past unreal** conditionals use the past perfect form of the verb in the *if* clause and *would have* plus the past participle in the result clause. *Could have* and *might have* are also possible in the result clause.

	If Clause	Result Clause
Future Real	If you *stay* up late tonight,	you *will be* very tired tomorrow.
	If we *have* enough time,	we *may go* to the movies on Friday.
Present Unreal	If you *stayed* up late every night,	you *would be* very tired.
	If we *had* more free time,	we *could go* out more often.
	If I *were* at the beach right now,	I *would swim* all day.
Past Unreal	If you *had stayed* up late last night,	you *would have been* very tired.
	If we *had had* more time last weekend,	we *might have gone* to the movies.

Many common verbs are irregular in their past and past participle forms.

PRESENT	PAST	PAST PARTICIPLE
become	became	become
begun	began	begun
bet	bet	bet
bite	bit	bitten
blow	blew	blown
break	broke	broken
bring	brought	brought
build	built	built
burst	burst	burst
buy	bought	bought
catch	caught	caught
choose	chose	chosen
come	came	come
cost	cost	cost
creep	crept	crept
cut	cut	cut
deal	dealt	dealt
dig	dug	dug
do	did	done
draw	drew	drawn
drink	drank	drunk
drive	drove	driven
eat	ate	eaten
fall	fell	fallen
feed	fed	fed
feel	felt	felt
fight	fought	fought
find	found	found
fly	flew	flown
forget	forgot	forgotten
freeze	froze	frozen
get	got	gotten
give	gave	given
go	went	gone
grow	grew	grown

PRESENT	PAST	PAST PARTICIPLE
hang	hung	hung
have	had	had
hear	heard	heard
hide	hid	hidden
hit	hit	hit
hold	held	held
hurt	hurt	hurt
keep	kept	kept
kneel	knelt	knelt
know	knew	known
lead	led	led
leave	left	left
lend	lent	lent
let	let	let
lie	lay	lain
lose	lost	lost
make	made	made
mean	meant	meant
meet	met	met
pay	paid	paid
put	put	put
read	read	read
ride	rode	ridden
ring	rang	rung
run	ran	run
say	said	said
see	saw	seen
sell	sold	sold
send	sent	sent
set	set	set
shake	shook	shaken
shine	shone	shone
shoot	shot	shot
shrink	shrank	shrunk

PRESENT	PAST	PAST PARTICIPLE
shut	shut	shut
sing	sang	sung
sink	sank	sunk
sit	sat	sat
sleep	slept	slept
speak	spoke	spoken
spend	spent	spent
spin	spun	spun
split	split	split
spread	spread	spread
spring	sprang	sprung
stand	stood	stood

PRESENT	PAST	PAST PARTICIPLE
steal	stole	stolen
sweep	swept	swept
swim	swam	swum
take	took	taken
teach	taught	taught
tear	tore	torn
tell	told	told
think	thought	thought
throw	threw	thrown
understand	understood	understood
wear	wore	worn
win	won	won
write	wrote	written

PAGE 1

A. 2. They're 3. It's 4. He's 5. It's 6. We're
7. She's 8. I'm 9. You're 10. They're

B. 2. is 3. is 4. are 5. is 6. are 7. are
8. is 9. is

PAGE 2

2. a. Is Ricardo angry with us? b. Ricardo isn't
angry with us. 3. a. Are Maya and Anna good
friends? b. Maya and Anna aren't good friends.
4. a. Is he very happy? b. He isn't very happy.
5. a. Are both sisters tall and athletic? b. Both
sisters aren't tall and athletic. 6. a. Is she a clever
girl? b. She isn't a clever girl. 7. a. Are they
members of our club? b. They aren't members of
our club. 8. a. Is he a good baseball player?
b. He isn't a good baseball player.

PAGE 3

2. was 3. were 4. were 5. were 6. was
7. were 8. were 9. were 10. was 11. were
12. was, was 13. was 14. was 15. was
16. were 17. were 18. was 19. was
20. were 21. was 22. was 23. were
24. were

PAGE 4

2. a. Were the doors closed? b. The doors
weren't closed. 3. a. Were the exercises difficult?
b. The exercises weren't difficult. 4. a. Was the
woman a stranger to her? b. The woman wasn't a
stranger to her. 5. a. Was it a beautiful day?
b. It wasn't a beautiful day. 6. a. Was the sea
very calm? b. The sea wasn't very calm.
7. a. Was he a tall man? b. He wasn't a tall man.
8. a. Were there many difficult exercises in the
lesson? b. There weren't many difficult exercises in
the lesson.

PAGE 5

2. is stopping 3. is ringing 4. you're wearing
5. is crossing 6. is starting 7. is sleeping
8. is trying 9. is making 10. are beginning
11. is having 12. is playing 13. they're living
14. is managing 15. is watching 16. They're
having 17. is watering 18. is spending

PAGE 6

2. a. Is it beginning to rain? b. It isn't beginning to
rain. 3. a. Is the sky growing dark? b. The sky
isn't growing dark. 4. a. Is he working for a new
company? b. He isn't working for a new company.
5. a. Is Pete cleaning the room now? b. Pete isn't
cleaning the room now. 6. a. Are the joggers
turning the corner? b. The joggers aren't turning
the corner. 7. a. Is she having lunch outside on
the patio? b. She isn't having lunch outside on the
patio. 8. a. Is Nora doing well in college?
b. Nora isn't doing well in college.

PAGE 7

2. was raining 3. was having 4. were traveling
5. was sleeping 6. was ordering 7. were
driving 8. was working 9. was taking
10. was talking 11. were staying 12. was
getting 13. was going 14. was shining
15. was watching 16. were driving 17. was
throwing 18. was sneezing

PAGE 8

2. John will be traveling 3. I'll be having
4. I'll be waiting 5. she'll be practicing 6. It'll
be raining 7. I'll be working 8. we'll be flying
9. He'll be watching 10. She'll be taking
11. he'll be studying 12. my parents will be
having 13. they'll be watching 14. I'll be
taking 15. my brother and I'll be driving

PAGE 9

2. comes 3. walk 4. play 5. eat 6. works
7. like 8. chases 9. works 10. sits
11. play 12. prepares 13. eat 14. likes
15. take 16. travel 17. visits 18. speaks
19. go 20. waters 21. jogs 22. changes

PAGE 10

A. 2. Ann does not like to study English.
3. They do not speak Chinese well. 4. The plane
does not leave at ten o'clock. 5. He does not
know French perfectly. 6. I do not live in this
neighborhood.

B. 2. I don't need air conditioning in my room.
3. We don't read a lot of books every summer.
4. I don't understand everything he says. 5. She
doesn't want to visit Mexico. 6. Sarah doesn't
enjoy classical music.

PAGE 11

2. Does he enjoy fishing? 3. Does she spend her
vacation in the mountains? 4. Do they come to
school by bus? 5. Does Andrew know how to
play soccer? 6. Do the children wake up at six

o'clock every morning?   7. Does he know a lot about politics?   8. Do they go to the park every afternoon?   9. Do they have many friends in that school?   10. Do both boys swim well?   11. Do they live on the outskirts of the city?

PAGE 12

2. listened   3. talked   4. wanted   5. lived
6. expected   7. lasted   8. changed   9. liked
10. waited   11. painted   12. arrived   13. watched
14. studied   15. mailed   16. learned
17. delivered   18. walked   19. cooked
20. waved   21. passed   22. turned off
23. moved

PAGE 13

2. told   3. sat   4. put   5. began   6. wrote
7. saw   8. cost   9. had   10. drank   11. gave
12. sold   13. heard   14. knew   15. felt
16. went   17. read   18. spoke, came   19. told

PAGE 14

A. 2. They did not fax us the story.   3. She did not put the bank statements on his desk.   4. We did not stay in Mexico City for two weeks.
5. I did not see Florence yesterday.

B. 2. I didn't know him very well.   3. You didn't sell your new modem.   4. Mr. Wood didn't speak to Beth about the exam.   5. She didn't come to the meeting alone.   6. We didn't sit together at the concert last night.

PAGE 15

2. Did Don give her some CDs for her birthday?
3. Did they stay in Japan all year?   4. Did she tell us about her trip?   5. Did he begin his university classes in September?   6. Did they go by plane?
7. Did she come home very late?   8. Did they go to the party together?   9. Did they know each other as children?   10. Did Rose work there for many years?   11. Did Mr. Stein feel better after his surgery?

PAGE 16

2. They'll see   3. I'll give   4. She'll help
5. will clean   6. will close   7. I'll leave   8. will find   9. You'll need   10. will do   11. will blow
12. We'll meet   13. I'll pay   14. You'll learn
15. We'll remain   16. she'll be   17. will pay
18. You'll spend   19. I'll make   20. you'll find
21. will give   22. will open

PAGE 17

A. 2. My girlfriend will not finish her degree next year.   3. I will not be back tomorrow.
4. The weather will not be cool tomorrow.
5. Tom will not be able to meet us this evening.

B. 2. She won't do well in that course.   3. Gina won't teach all the computer courses.   4. Jim and I won't sign the contract tomorrow.   5. They won't finish the work in April.   6. The meeting won't last an hour.

PAGE 18

A. 2. Will Ned come back at three o'clock?
3. Will the shop be open at six o'clock?
4. Will it cost sixty dollars to fix the microwave?   5. Will the plant die without sunshine?

B. 2. When will they pay their bill?   3. What time will the meeting begin?   4. How long will the fireworks last?   5. What will Lucy buy for her husband?

PAGE 19

2. We're going to have   3. I'm going to go
4. He's going to leave   5. She's going to visit
6. You're going to speak   7. is going to study
8. is going to take   9. They're going to wait
10. We're going to fly   11. is going to study
12. We're going to get   13. are going to go
14. She's going to leave   15. They're going to tear down   16. is going to go   17. They're going to sell   18. is going to take   19. They're going to buy   20. are going to do   21. is going to help

PAGE 20

2. a. Is Rose going to take a vacation? b. Rose is not going to take a vacation.   3. a. Are we going to go to the movies tonight? b. We're not going to go to the movies tonight.   4. a. Is he going to start working there on Monday? b. He's not going to start working there on Monday.   5. a. Are they going to pay him a good salary? b. They're not going to pay him a good salary.   6. a. Is Carmen going to move to California next month? b. Carmen is not going to move to California next month.   7. a. Is Henry going to travel to Asia on business? b. Henry is not going to travel to Asia on business.   8. a. Is she going to spend the weekend in Connecticut? b. She's not going to spend the weekend in Connecticut.

PAGE 21

2. We've finished   3. He's visited   4. She's returned   5. I've lost   6. We've been   7. I've done   8. We've learned   9. have been   10. I've heard   11. We've lent   12. has gone   13. has taught   14. She's seen   15. has tried   16. He's begun   17. have grown   18. They've been   19. has visited

PAGE 22

2. a. Has she been there for many years? b. She hasn't been there for many years.   3. a. Have they waited there a long time? b. They haven't waited there a long time.   4. a. Has the movie been seen by millions of people? b. The movie hasn't been seen by millions of people.   5. a. Have Mr. and Mrs. Sato studied English? b. Mr. and Mrs. Sato haven't studied English.   6. a. Has Alan been absent? b. Alan hasn't been absent.   7. a. Have they found the money? b. They haven't found the money.   8. a. Has he been the best student all year? b. He hasn't been the best student all year.

PAGE 23

2. He's been selling cars for many years.
3. They've been living in Europe since last spring.
4. Susan has been sleeping for more than ten hours.   5. It's been raining all day long.   6. My brother has been studying English for many years.
7. She's been catching fish in that stream for years.
8. He's been teaching English for ten years.   9. The two nations have been quarreling for many years.

PAGE 24

2. had looked   3. had worked   4. had caught
5. had prepared   6. had written   7. had gone
8. had worked   9. had ordered   10. had left
11. had seen   12. had stopped   13. had heard
14. had been   15. had misdirected   16. had been
17. had visited   18. had eaten   19. had passed
20. had left

PAGE 25

2. had been watching   3. had been living   4. had been speeding   5. had been swimming   6. had been lying   7. had been working   8. had been going   9. had been running   10. had been playing
11. had been walking   12. had not been sleeping

PAGE 26

2. will have died   3. will have finished   4. will have left   5. will have gone   6. will have finished   7. will have been   8. will have forgotten   9. will have learned   10. will have forgotten   11. will have seen   12. will have arrived   13. will have finished   14. will have lost   15. will have done   16. will have completed   17. will have eaten   18. will have changed

PAGE 27

2. is teaching   3. was working   4. will have/are going to have   5. came   6. was coming, met, asked   7. have been   8. is playing   9. had seen   10. have read   11. will have completed   12. came, was leaving   13. shone, was shining   14. begins   15. go   16. has studied/has been studying   17. studied   18. will come/is going to come   19. was studying   20. jumped   21. had called, had left   22. fell, was crossing

PAGE 28

2. We didn't go to the movies last night.   3. You shouldn't tell him.   4. He shouldn't go there soon.
5. I haven't lived there for many years.   6. They weren't supposed to leave yesterday.   7. She can't speak French perfectly.   8. The mechanic won't be back by eight o'clock.   9. He didn't have to work late last night.   10. My friend doesn't live in Los Angeles.   11. She isn't the best student in our class.   12. You may not park here.   13. There weren't many students absent from class yesterday.   14. They weren't driving very fast at the time.

PAGE 29

2. Can Mr. Ralston speak Chinese fluently?
3. Should she spend more time at home?   4. May he sit in this chair?   5. Can they meet us in Los Angeles?   6. Can't her brother-in-law drive?
7. Should Ruth eat less candy?   8. Should you tell her the truth?   9. Should we speak to her about it?   10. May they leave now?   11. Can the entire tour group go by van?   12. Should you send them an e-mail message?   13. Should he work at home?   14. May they wait in the office?

PAGE 30

2. How many students are there in this class?
3. Where may she wait?   4. What time did the plane arrive?   5. What time is it now?   6. How did he go to Chicago?   7. What time should she leave?   8. Where are they right now?   9. How much did the book cost?   10. Where do they work now?   11. How long did her supervisor live in Tokyo?   12. What time did he get up this morning?   13. How long did they sit in the park?
14. How well does she understand English?

PAGE 31

2. They're 3. I'll 4. I've 5. We'll 6. She'll
7. We're 8. They're 9. It's 10. It's
11. They've 12. It's 13. There's 14. She's
15. He's 16. You're 17. I'm 18. There's
19. They'll 20. It's 21. You'll 22. I'd
23. They've 24. I'd 25. She'll 26. He's

PAGE 32

2. a. Yes, she does. b. No, she doesn't. 3. a. Yes,
I have. b. No, I haven't. 4. a. Yes, it is. b. No, it
isn't. 5. a. Yes, they will. b. No, they won't.
6. a. Yes, they are. b. No, they aren't. 7. a. Yes,
she did. b. No, she didn't. 8. a. Yes, it was.
b. No, it wasn't. 9. a. Yes, it is. b. No, it isn't.
10. a. Yes, we should. b. No, we shouldn't.
11. a. Yes, you may. b. No, you may not.
12. a. Yes, he can. b. No, he can't. 13. a. Yes, it
did. b. No, it didn't.

PAGE 33

2. doesn't she 3. was it 4. has it 5. isn't it
6. aren't you 7. won't there 8. didn't she
9. hasn't it 10. will you 11. doesn't he
12. did you 13. can she 14. don't they
15. aren't you 16. don't you 17. are they
18. could he 19. didn't I 20. has it

PAGE 34

A. 2. to be enjoying 3. to be doing 4. to be
spending 5. to be trying 6. to be learning 7. to
be working 8. to be having

B. 2. to have met 3. to have arrived 4. to
have enjoyed 5. to have understood 6. to have
caught 7. to have missed 8. to have been

PAGE 35

2. wait 3. to give 4. look/to look 5. come
6. to leave 7. leave 8. fall 9. wait 10. touch
11. take 12. to know 13. play 14. write/to
write 15. laugh 16. to be 17. play

PAGE 36

2. The heavy box was carried by him. 3. The
president was recognized immediately. 4. My
umbrella has been stolen. 5. The merchandise
will be delivered in the morning. 6. The portrait
had already been finished. 7. The work was
finished in time. 8. The cries of wolves were heard
in the distance. 9. A young tiger was found in the
open field by the rangers. 10. The tiger was
frightened by the rangers' truck.

PAGE 37

2. We were taught two languages. 3. We were
sent an invitation. 4. The man was given a reward
of a hundred dollars. 5. She will be sent flowers.
6. We were shown the principal spots of interest.
7. I was told the news last night. 8. Everyone has
been asked the same question. 9. The police were
given the information. 10. Each of us has been
promised a raise.

PAGE 38

2. He was being sent to school. 3. The case is
being argued now. 4. A new subway is being
built in that city. 5. Some chairs are being put in
that room now, aren't they? 6. A letter is being
faxed now, isn't it? 7. The building across the
street is being torn down. 8. The plants are being
watered. 9. The verdict is being discussed now.
10. Many new buildings were being constructed in
Caracas when I was there. 11. The streets are
being kept much cleaner now.

PAGE 39

2. The box should be taken to Philadelphia.
3. The engine has to be started first. 4. A new
group may be organized. 5. My appointment
ought to be canceled. 6. The meeting cannot be
held in that room. 7. The computer may be
delivered while you're out. 8. Her credit card has
to be paid by the first of the month. 9. The other
bills must be paid by the end of the month.
10. The plants ought to be watered once a week.

PAGE 40

2. My history teacher was not born in
Philadelphia. 3. The garden was not watered.
4. The mail is not delivered at ten o'clock.
5. His car was not stolen from in front of his house.
6. The goods will not be delivered on Wednesday.
7. The thief was not sent to prison. 8. This door
cannot be opened with this key. 9. The children
were not put to bed. 10. The new cell phones
will not be delivered tomorrow. 11. The table
has not been moved.

PAGE 41

2. Can the music be heard in the next room?
3. Is this company owned by its employees? 4. Is
this class taught by Professor Parks? 5. Should
the house be painted soon? 6. Will Dr. Schmidt
be assisted by Dr. Fleurat? 7. Will the stores be
closed early tomorrow? 8. Has the electricity
been turned off? 9. Were both doors opened with

the superintendent's key? 10. Was he very much discouraged by his failures? 11. Were they surprised by his behavior? 12. Was her arm broken in three places?

PAGE 42

2. may 3. can 4. could 5. preferred 6. would 7. meant 8. has 9. will 10. were crossing 11. was going 12. would 13. is 14. was 15. doesn't 16. kept 17. had died 18. wanted 19. had 20. remembered

PAGE 43

2. Nick said that it was getting late. 3. He said that we would have to hurry. 4. Watson said that it looked like rain. 5. Monique said that she had seen that movie. 6. Sue said that she could leave them a message. 7. Mr. Kovacs said that he had to go to the customs office. 8. The man said that he needed more time to complete the project.

PAGE 44

2. Ms. Cruz asked if/whether I liked New York. 3. She asked what time it was. 4. Melanie asked where Busch Gardens was. 5. He asked if/whether Paolo sang well. 6. The man asked how I was. 7. My professor asked where the meeting was. 8. She asked why I was late. 9. The teacher asked where Andorra was.

PAGE 45

2. They told me not to go. 3. I told him to leave me alone. 4. You told him to close the door. 5. She told me not to turn off the computer. 6. Anne told David to drive carefully. 7. He told her to think it over. 8. They told me to come back later. 9. My father told us not to jump on the bed. 10. He told her not to come late. 11. My doctor told him to take two aspirins and plenty of vitamin C.

PAGE 46

A. 2. Sarah had her sweater pressed. 3. Larry had his old van overhauled. 4. I must have my printer fixed. 5. The front office had those letters mailed. 6. We must have our apartment painted.

B. 2. Mrs. Jackson got her office painted. 3. She is going to get her nails manicured. 4. You should get the roof repaired. 5. I will get the water tank filled. 6. My mother got her rose garden weeded.

PAGE 47

2. How handsome he is! 3. What a bright young lady her oldest daughter is! 4. How quickly they have learned English! 5. What a beautiful new car you have! 6. How well Helen drives! 7. How tall Ryan has grown! 8. What a charming city Paris is! 9. What good taste she has! 10. What a gorgeous home they have!

PAGE 48

2. She thinks he does know the song. 3. Fred didn't come, but he did call. 4. I did like it very much. 5. Do come back later. 6. Do visit us again sometime. 7. She does enjoy her lessons. 8. We did do these exercises. 9. I don't like movies, but I do like the theater. 10. Do tell us all about it. 11. He did try to please us. 12. We don't make much money, but we do have a lot of fun.

PAGE 49

2. I don't think so. 3. I believe so. 4. I don't think so. 5. I believe so. 6. I'm afraid so. 7. I believe so. 8. I hope so. 9. I think so. 10. I believe so. 11. I don't believe so.

PAGE 50

2. there is! 3. they have! 4. he must! 5. he has! 6. she is! 7. it is! 8. she is! 9. she does! 10. there are! 11. it is! 12. it can! 13. he can! 14. they will! 15. it is! 16. they are! 17. you are! 18. it is!

PAGE 51

2. does 3. did 4. are 5. will 6. did 7. has 8. did 9. is 10. will 11. did 12. is 13. have 14. did 15. are 16. do 17. were 18. is 19. will 20. does

PAGE 52

A. 2. He didn't go, and I didn't either. 3. He didn't study, and Marc didn't either. 4. She won't be there, and her sister won't either. 5. Dolores hasn't heard the tape, and you haven't either. 6. You can't speak Latin, and Desmond can't either.

B. 2. Marta doesn't know them, and neither do we. 3. Your watch doesn't have the right time, and neither does my watch/mine. 4. She hasn't seen him, and neither have I. 5. Paula never rests, and neither does Mindy. 6. He wouldn't say that, and neither would I.

2. is supposed to come   3. were supposed to deliver   4. was supposed to send   5. was supposed to send   6. am supposed to write   7. is supposed to be   8. is supposed to take   9. is supposed to be   10. was supposed to call   11. is supposed to be   12. are supposed to read   13. is supposed to call   14. am supposed to arrive   15. are supposed to meet   16. is supposed to spend   17. was supposed to publish   18. am supposed to get up   19. are supposed to put   20. is supposed to prepare   21. are supposed to go   22. is supposed to be

2. He used to work here.   3. She used to come to class on time.   4. Monica used to be an industrious student.   5. He used to ride the subway to work.   6. Colette used to bring me flowers every day.   7. Mike used to play the trumpet very well.
8. He used to study hard.   9. My adviser used to help me very much.   10. I used to live on Forty-sixth Street.   11. Her father used to go to that college.   12. I used to know her well.

2. a. used to b. are used to   3. a. used to b. is used to   4. a. am used to b. used to   5. a. used to b. is used to   6. a. are used to b. used to
7. a. used to b. is used to   8. a. used to b. am used to   9. a. used to b. are used to   10. a. used to b. is used to   11. a. is used to b. used to
12. a. used to b. is used to

2. He'd better see a doctor.   3. Sue had better rest for a while.   4. You'd better take private lessons.   5. They'd better save a little money.
6. Peter had better not mention this to anyone.
7. You'd better eat more fruits and vegetables.
8. She'd better stop seeing him.   9. Dennis had better memorize these facts.   10. Your lawyer had better call my lawyer.   11. We'd better not give them too many details.

2. She'd rather come back later.   3. He'd rather watch TV.   4. They'd rather walk to school.
5. Dan would rather do all his homework before he leaves school.   6. I'd rather stay home tonight and watch TV.   7. Betty would rather drive a big car.   8. We'd rather spend the summer at home instead of in the country.   9. He'd rather not speak to her about the matter again.   10. Marie

would rather not mention it to anyone.   11. She'd rather study in this class.

2. If you should pass a mailbox, please mail this letter.   3. If that letter should arrive, bring it to my office at once.   4. If Dad should hear about it, I won't be able to go.   5. If you should hear the rumor, don't believe it.   6. If the electricity should go off, we will have to work in the dark.   7. If the weather should turn cold, we will have to cancel the game.   8. If the dog should bite her, she'll probably sue us.   9. If a police officer should see you driving that way, you'll get a ticket.   10. If you should break the glass, you'll have to buy another.

A. 2. rises   3. raises   4. raised   5. rose
6. risen   7. raise   8. rose

B. 2. sat   3. set   4. sit   5. set   6. set
7. sitting   8. sit

A. 2. lay   3. lay   4. lain   5. laid   6. lying
7. laid   8. Lie   9. laid

B. 2. rose   3. rises   4. set   5. laid   6. lie
7. raise   8. rising   9. lying

2. surprised   3. interested   4. interesting
5. disgusting   6. disgusted   7. pleased
8. embarrassed   9. exciting   10. confused
11. soothed   12. energizing   13. confusing
14. excited   15. soothing

2. Having finished the work, she left.   3. Seeing her, I cried with joy.   4. Having spoken to her, he was very happy.   5. Having heard her explanation, he had to forgive her.   6. Leaving the party, we ran into Joyce and Tom.   7. Having left here, they went to another party.   8. Having stayed outside all day without a coat, Martha became ill.   9. Being so busy at work these days, I don't have much time to spend with my friends.

2. driving   3. going   4. waiting   5. buying
6. traveling   7. coming   8. holding

9. receiving   10. painting   11. hitting
12. taking   13. going   14. making
15. breaking   16. turning   17. going
18. working   19. planting   20. cleaning

2. for arriving   3. in hearing   4. for trying
5. of losing   6. of leaving   7. for helping
8. from meeting   9. in speaking   10. about
taking   11. on driving   12. to meeting   13. of
working   14. for missing   15. of finishing
16. of mentioning   17. of seeing   18. in doing
19. from continuing   20. for washing   21. for
choosing   22. in helping

A. 2. Playing   3. Painting, drawing   4. Walking
5. Taking   6. Working   7. Waking up
8. Living   9. Starting   10. Swimming, jogging

B. 2. has been   3. takes   4. was   5. helps
6. is   7. has been   8. is   9. improves   10. is

A. 1. despite   2. despite   3. despite   4. despite
5. Despite

B. 1. in spite of   2. In spite of   3. in spite of
4. In spite of   5. in spite of

C. 1.–8. Individual answers

2. because   3. although   4. although   5. because
6. because   7. although   8. because   9. although
10. although   11. because   12. because
13. Because   14. Although   15. although
16. although   17. because   18. Because
19. Although   20. although

2. such a   3. So   4. so   5. so   6. such a
7. such an   8. so   9. such   10. such   11. so
12. so   13. so   14. such   15. such a   16. so

2. The last lesson was difficult, but this one is easy.
3. This chair is very comfortable, but that one is
not.   4. They have two black cats and three white
ones.   5. You were asking about a black notebook.
Is this the one that you lost?   6. I like all games,
but tennis and basketball are the ones I like most.
7. We find that it is more fun to take several short
trips than one long one.   8. There were boats of
all sizes in the bay, big ones and little ones.
9. We took pictures of everything, but the ones
we took of the gardens turned out best.
10. This computer disk is defective; please give me
a new one.

2. thirsty   3. foolish   4. quarrelsome   5. manly
6. childish   7. greedy   8. wiry   9. talented
10. hourly   11. sunny   12. cloudy
13. revolutionary   14. hungry   15. daily
16. peaceful   17. needy   18. dirty
19. cultural   20. beautiful   21. dead
22. flowery   23. weekly   24. monthly   25. tasty
26. summery   27. wintry   28. Egyptian   29. Irish
30. Chinese   31. Swedish   32. Swiss
33. Turkish   34. Spanish   35. Mexican
36. Japanese   37. Canadian   38. Indian
39. Greek   40. Brazilian

2. anger   3. depth   4. happiness   5. height
6. convenience   7. ugliness   8. possibility
9. width   10. sarcasm   11. absence   12. danger
13. weakness   14. strength   15. emphasis
16. silence   17. intelligence   18. generosity
19. jealousy   20. anxiety   21. desperation
22. greatness   23. beauty   24. roughness
25. death   26. loudness   27. selfishness
28. cynic/cynicism   29. presence   30. deceit
31. bitterness   32. sweetness   33. electricity
34. dryness   35. heat   36. bashfulness
37. pride   38. dreariness   39. truth   40. clarity

3. dependence   4. operation   5. education
6. action   7. argument   8. confidence
9. creation   10. imagination   11. reflection
12. concentration   13. enjoyment   14. discussion
15. suggestion   16. satisfaction   17. organization
18. translation   19. motivation   20. preference
21. existence   22. agreement   23. improvement
24. conversation   25. announcement
26. annoyance   27. requirement
28. encouragement   29. management
30. preparation   31. exertion   32. gratification
33. connection   34. corruption   35. magnification
36. settlement   37. deterrence/deterrent
38. payment   39. statement   40. declaration

3. to undress   4. unclear   5. irregular
6. impossible   7. unfriendly   8. to disobey

9. to dislike   10. uncommon   11. to misspell
12. nonfiction   13. atypical   14. incomplete
15. improbable   16. to dissatisfy   17. to unpack
18. unknown   19. unemployed   20. irresponsible
21. independent   22. unfinished   23. inconsiderate
24. to misunderstand   25. uninteresting
26. unconscious   27. unskilled   28. nonexistent
29. nonviolence   30. to displease   31. unpopular
32. insincere   33. imperfect   34. unequal
35. insensitive   36. unofficial   37. to misplace
38. to disassemble   39. uncomfortable   40. to
disagree

Page 74

3. mathematician   4. educator   5. writer
6. artist   7. novelist   8. journalist   9. baker
10. gardener   11. librarian   12. politician
13. vegetarian   14. painter   15. drummer
16. actor/actress   17. skier   18. driver
19. dancer   20. biologist   21. instructor
22. pharmacist   23. pianist   24. economist

Page 75

2. as far as   3. as far as   4. until   5. as far as
6. until   7. As far as   8. until   9. as far as
10. until   11. as far as   12. as far as   13. as
far as   14. until   15. until   16. as far as
17. until   18. as far as   19. until   20. until

Page 76

2. I saw him on TV yesterday.   3. She usually
comes to meetings on time.   4. Luisa prepared her
lesson well last night.   5. I often watch music
videos.   6. My uncle generally reads *Time* magazine
every week.   7. We usually go for a walk in the
park on Sunday.   8. My friends and I went for a
stroll in the park last Sunday.   9. She never takes an
early train.   10. I seldom drink milk.

Page 77

2. anymore   3. anymore   4. still   5. anymore
6. still   7. anymore   8. anymore   9. still,
anymore   10. still   11. still   12. anymore
13. still   14. still, anymore   15. still, still
16. anymore   17. still   18. still, anymore
19. anymore, still

Page 78

2. Nobody else helped him with the work.
3. You must ask somebody else about it.   4. Who
else knows the combination?   5. They have never
sold that merchandise anywhere else.   6. Did you
see anything else that you liked?   7. Let's do

something else tonight besides watch TV.
8. I didn't tell anybody else about it.   9. How
else can I paint the room?

Page 79

2. Whoever   3. whenever   4. whatever
5. whatever   6. whenever   7. whatever
8. Whoever   9. wherever   10. Whenever
11. wherever/whenever   12. whenever
13. wherever   14. whichever, whenever
15. whenever   16. whenever   17. Whenever
18. Whoever   19. Whatever

Page 80

2. many   3. much   4. a lot of   5. few
6. little   7. little   8. few   9. much   10. few
11. little   12. a lot of   13. many   14. much
15. many   16. a lot of   17. many   18. much
19. many

Page 81

2. a little   3. few   4. a little   5. few   6. a few
7. A few   8. little   9. a little   10. few
11. a few   12. few   13. little   14. few

Page 82

2. Nick's   3. are   4. me   5. they   6. much
7. me   8. themselves   9. a   10. an   11. an
12. always   13. set   14. exciting   15. them
16. a   17. a   18. an   19. her   20. me
21. excited   22. ourselves   23. yours   24. my

Page 83

2. about/of   3. in   4. to/with   5. for   6. to
7. for   8. at   9. from   10. by/about   11. to
12. to   13. at   14. to/at   15. in   16. from
17. at/about   18. at/for   19. from   20. from

Page 84

2. The woman you were speaking to is my teacher.
3. That is the store I lost my purse in.   4. She is
the kind of salesperson it is difficult to get away
from.   5. The adviser you should speak to is
Dr. Kojima.   6. It is a subject we will never
agree on.   7. The thing they were arguing about
was really of little importance.   8. It is a place
you will feel at home in.   9. It was Charles I had
to wait so long for.   10. It was Jack he
borrowed the money from.   11. The room we
study in is on the second floor.

PAGE 85

2. effect   3. effects   4. advise   5. into   6. stole
7. somewhat   8. affected   9. advice

PAGE 86

2. taught   3. have I   4. beside   5. teach
6. beside   7. taught   8. besides   9. did he
mention   10. learned   11. could you   12. was
he   13. seen   14. learned

PAGE 87

2. no   3. won   4. not   5. spilled   6. poured
7. Not   8. poured   9. won

PAGE 88

2. The, the, the   3. a, a, a, The, a, _____
4. _____, _____   5. the, _____, the   6. a, the
7. The, _____, the, _____   8. the, the, _____
9. _____, The   10. _____, the, the   11. _____,
the, the   12. the, The   13. _____, the
14. _____, _____, _____, _____, _____
15. the, _____   16. The, _____, _____   17. The
18. The, _____   19. _____, the   20. _____,
_____, the, the, the   21. a, _____, an   22. _____,
the, the

PAGE 89

1. We study history, mathematics, geography, and
reading.   2. Sue Bielski, the mechanic, repaired
our car and also fixed our refrigerator.   3. Mike
Madison, the head of the company, will see you on
Sunday.   4. The governor, in the first place, did
not want the action.   5. He was born in Scranton,
Pennsylvania, on March 23, 1980, and he has lived
there ever since.   6. We cannot, after all, live
forever.   7. By the way, do you remember Mrs.
Jackson's telephone number?   8. Sue Brown,
Henry's cousin, is visiting him in New York.
9. Where were you, Miss Lyons, on the morning
of June 26, 2003?   10. The old Amos Building,
a famous landmark of the town, was recently torn
down. As a matter of fact, it was torn down on
February 12, Lincoln's Birthday.   11. The most
popular summer sports are tennis, swimming, and
hiking.   12. Yesterday, I met my schoolmates Tom
Beck, Ruth Sanchez, and Randy Owens.   13. The
last time I saw them was on August 3, 2003.

PAGE 90

1. If it rains, we may have to postpone our trip.
2. I may, if the weather is bad, cancel the class trip.
3. We may have to postpone our trip if it rains.

4. When he protested so vigorously, we withdrew
our proposal.   5. Because he was so widely read,
he had a comprehensive grasp of the issues.   6. As
soon as we had closed the shop, we went home.
7. Because he had been ill, he asked to be excused
from all assignments.   8. If Monica wanted, she
could be a very good student.   9. After Yoshiko
got her visa, she bought an airline ticket.   10. He
never studied any foreign language when he was in
high school.   11. When he was in high school, he
never studied any foreign language.   12. He never,
when he was in high school, studied any foreign
language.   13. Although she was a skilled engineer,
she did not know anything about road building.
14. Natasha, as was easily seen from her speech,
was a woman of strong opinions.   15. He took the
kettle, an antique he had bought in England, off the
stove.   16. When the last guest had gone, we
looked at the pile of dirty dishes, sighed, and got to
work.   17. If you stopped making excuses and just
did the work, you would be finished in no time.

PAGE 91

1. Barbara, who is quite smart, deserves to pass.
2. Any student who is lazy does not deserve to
pass.   3. Any girl who has good acting ability can
audition for the part of the heroine.   4. Angela,
who has good acting ability, was selected for the
part of the heroine.   5. Daniel's hands, feet, and
face, which were covered with mud, were washed
by Mother.   6. Any passenger who enters the
engine room does so at his or her own risk.   7. The
person who said that was mistaken.   8. Eva, who
told the story, was obviously misinformed.
9. Wednesday, when my brother is usually out of
town, will be a good day to call.   10. Ms. Rubio,
who was in the real estate business, decided to
promote Glen Acres, which was formerly a swamp.
11. The fellow who was laughing was clearly the
perpetrator of the joke.   12. His great love for
nature, which he acquired during his childhood,
showed itself in his curiosity about any bird flying
through his garden.   13. The profit which you
can expect on so cheap an article is very small.
14. We heard a noise that resembled the cry of an
injured animal.   15. The George Washington
Bridge, which spans the Hudson River, has been
very successful financially.   16. Kyle, unlike his
brother Josh, has brown hair, blue eyes, and a light
complexion.

PAGE 92

1. Chicago is my favorite city, but Philadelphia offers
more advantages.   2. Fools need advice; only wise
men profit by it.   3. The general manager will talk

to you soon and will give you the information. 4. Alec is a very good automobile mechanic, and his prices are low. 5. I had the jacket for a week, but then finally I returned it. 6. She kept the book for a long time, but she finally returned it. 7. Bill had the ring; then he gave it to Joe. 8. Marcia didn't go, but Colleen did. 9. Mary was highly pleased with the results; therefore, she showed her pleasure and gave us all a day off. 10. Lou was pleased with the results, but Mr. Martin obviously wasn't. 11. Cowards die many times, but a brave man dies only once. 12. Marianne was cautious, but Henry bet on the black horse and won more than a hundred dollars. 13. Tom plays the bass, and Dennis plays the acoustic guitar. 14. I like board games; my sister likes computer games. 15. He was tattered and dirty, but he ate like a gentleman. 16. My brother or my mother will help you and will gladly show you the way.

PAGE 93

1. The changes which we are planning will soon be completed. 2. Jenny and Alice came into the room, looked around, whispered to each other, and then walked out. 3. William's store, which sells many fancy groceries, was recently repainted, and as a consequence, it now looks very nice. 4. "I am sure, Sophie," said Henry, "you will like our new summer place, which was built by the local company." 5. "Of course, Father, it's a pity," said Ellen, "that people don't appreciate the excellent work that you have done here." 6. We drove from Harrisburg to Albany, which is the capital of New York state. 7. Mary and Ellen stopped and watched Henry and Joseph running and jumping. 8. We, Mary, Ethel, and I, considered going, but later we changed our minds and decided to stay at home and rest. 9. The woman whom we saw yesterday was Don Gray's sister, Terry Nelson, who is a psychologist. 10. Saturday, Jan. 16, was the coldest day that we had, but the next day seemed even colder to me. 11. Everyone got into the van, we started out, and soon we were on the freeway. 12. At 11:00, Rex adjourned the meeting, no decision having been reached by that time. 13. "I believe," said the visitor, "that Mr. Davis should be notified at once, yet we all realize that the duty is not a pleasant one." 14. Strangely enough, Heather and Jennifer came into the room, looked at the table, sat down, and began to read. 15. She is very intelligent, but the lack of a diploma would prevent her from entering any college, even one of low standards. 16. They didn't notice the mail carrier; he came by every day at that time. 17. Having never traveled abroad, she sought our advice on hotels, transportation, money exchange, and much more besides that. 18. Louise never admitted when she was wrong, being unjustifiably sure of her own judgments.